BILL GATES

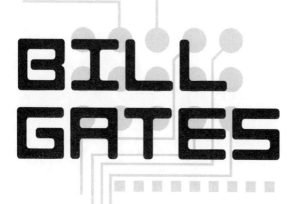

a twentieth-century life by
MARC ARONSON

VIKING

VIKING
Published by Penguin Group
Penguin Young Readers Group, 345 Hudson Street, New York, New York 10014, U.S.A.

Penguin Books Ltd, Registered Offices: 80 Strand, London WC2R 0RL, England

First published in 2009 by Viking, a division of Penguin Young Readers Group

10 9 8 7 6 5 4 3 2 1

Photo credits
Page 5: Courtesy of the Computer History Museum ◘ **Page 14:** Courtesy Jeff Miller/University of Wisconsin–Madison ◘ **Page 21:** Courtesy Benjamin Benschneider/*The Seattle Times* ◘ **Page 29:** Courtesy of the Museum of History & Industry. All rights reserved. neg #1965.3598.26.91 ◘ **Page 39:** Courtesy Lakeside School ◘ **Page 43:** Courtesy Lakeside School ◘ **Page 67:** Copyright *Popular Electronics*, 1975, courtesy of the Computer History Museum ◘ **Page 75:** Courtesy Barry Wong/*The Seattle Times* ◘ **Page 86:** Courtesy Richard S. Heyza/*The Seattle Times* ◘ **Page 94:** Courtesy Porsche werkfoto ◘ **Page 101:** Courtesy Charles Simonyi ◘ **Page 117:** Courtesy Microsoft ◘ **Page 119:** Courtesy Charles Simonyi ◘ **Page 151:** Courtesy Mike Siegel/*The Seattle Times* ◘ **Page 155:** Courtesy Steve Ringman/*The Seattle Times* ◘ **Page 173:** Courtesy of the Computer History Museum

LIBRARY OF CONGRESS CATALOGING-IN-PUBLICATION DATA
Aronson, Marc.
Up close : Bill Gates / by Marc Aronson.
p. cm.
title: Bill Gates
ISBN 978-0-670-06348-2 (hardcover)
1. Gates, Bill, date- 2. Businessmen—United States—Biography. 3. Success in business.
4. Computer software industry—United States—History. 5. Microsoft Corporation—History.
I. Title. II. Title: Bill Gates.
HD9696.63.U62G3715 2008
338.7'610053092—dc22
[B]
2008015552

Printed in the U.S.A.
Set in Goudy
Book design by Jim Hoover

To the next generation of digital pioneers. Sergei Diaghilev, the great impresario of twentieth-century art and dance, famously urged artists to "astonish me"—I expect no less from you.

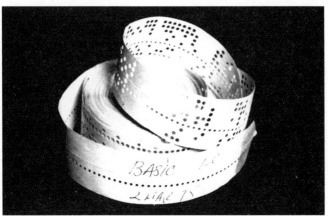

Basic 1.0 for the Altair—the program that launched Microsft.

CONTENTS

BILL GATES

FOREWORD

BILL GATES IS one of the richest people in the world. When adults talk about Bill, the cofounder and long-time head of the computer software giant Microsoft, they either admire or detest him. They want to learn business secrets from him, or they see him as a thief who turned the digital world into an evil inversion of what it should have been, where inferior products drive out better ones. Then they have to account for the billions of dollars he now gives to good causes each year, which complicates the picture. *Who is Bill Gates?* they ask themselves. The hard-bitten tycoon whose business has been called a monopoly by courts in America and Europe, or the global philanthropist? But when I asked a teenage friend what he wanted to know about Bill, he instantly replied: "How did he do it?" How could a smart teenager use his interests, his drive, his insights, his passions to become so wealthy?

I saw at once that my friend was right—that is what I had to write about. And yet I am an adult. I could not help also asking those big questions, those character questions, along the way. So I have tried to give you two books in one. As I describe Bill's early life and career I am simultaneously offering a biography and a "How To" book. I explain what he did in order to give a sense of how he did it—what it takes to Be Like Bill. There are lengthy biographies that continue the story through each year of Microsoft's history: each launch, each product, each competitor and court case. I found some of them—especially *Gates*, by Stephen Manes and Paul Andrews—extremely helpful, but I don't aim to be that comprehensive. After I explain Bill's rise, I leapfrog through his career to the present, touching down on key moments.

I have written this book for someone a bit like me—a person who uses computers all of the time but has little or no technical knowledge. I thought keeping that reader in mind would allow people who are curious about Bill and his billions to enjoy the book without feeling lost in unfamiliar terms. It occurred to me that perhaps teenagers today would be so accustomed to computers that they'd find my approach too simplistic. But when I sent the manuscript out to teenagers to read, I found that, while there were a few computer fans who were real experts, most teenagers use computers without being familiar with technical terms or the history of the machines. So I have added a kind of narrative glossary at the end. You can use it either to check on terms that you don't know or to delve a bit deeper into the computer history I've left out of the main narrative.

Writing a biography is a set of decisions—what to put in, what to leave out, and how to tell the story. I have chosen this "How To"-and-glossary form as the best way to write about Bill. If nothing else, I hope this book shows that choosing how to frame a biography, the format you use, can be as creative a decision as how you write a sentence.

Bill Gates as a surprise guest speaker at the University of Wisconsin–Madison. Though he did not finish college, he has always enjoyed challenging, and being challenged by, smart people.

INTRODUCTION

BILL GATES'S STORY is the story of the making of the world we live in. For those of you determined to follow in his footsteps and dominate the next generation of business, I'll offer what guidance I can. For those who just want to understand a titan who shaped our time—just as Thomas Edison, John D. Rockefeller, Andrew Carnegie, or Henry Ford did theirs—I'll give you my best insights. (Bill decorated his Microsoft office with pictures of Edison, Ford, Albert Einstein, and Leonardo da Vinci—so he is clearly aware of the comparisons.) For better or for worse, we all live in Bill's world. Here's why.

When Bill Gates was born in 1955, no one in the world owned a personal computer. There were none available for anyone to buy. There were computers, but these were massive things owned by governments, universities, and large businesses; kept in separate rooms; and fussed over by scientists in white lab coats. FORTRAN, ALGOL, and COBOL—the languages often used to program these whirring hunks of machinery—were just being invented. A keyboard was on a typewriter—a manual typewriter. You could only correct a mistake by slipping in a strip of white tape and typing over the incorrect letter, thus erasing it, then typing the right letter. IM was a mistake in punctuation. Fonts were known only to typesetters in print shops. A window always had a pane of glass. A mouse was a rodent. No one had ever sent an e-mail. There was no Web, thus no Web sites, search engines, or blogs. Games were played with people, not joysticks. Telephones were black and relatively heavy, had large round dials with holes in them, and only worked if they were directly linked to a phone line. If news happened after the last morning newspaper was printed, you might hear it on the radio (but there were no all-news stations), or see it on TV (but there were no live broadcasts from spots outside the studio), or read it in the afternoon

Allen warned and Bill himself discovered at Harvard, there are people with higher IQs. *He is extremely hard-working*—though his own company would not hire workaholic drudges, unless they were also very smart (see above). *He likes being around smart people*, is not threatened by them, and thrives in a world where everyone is competing to do his or her best. *He is determined*—some call that callous, driven, inhuman. Ever since he was a teenager, he has been *shrewd and known how to size up a deal and write it up with just the right legal wording*, though some say the deals are one-sided. Most of all, *Bill excels at dominating the near future*: he has the gift of seeing what is coming and what is about to be, and then he focuses everything—his intelligence, his relentless efforts, his team of bright people, his determination, and his deal-making charm and lawyerly skill—on making sure that he and his company dominate that next invention, product, or market. Others conquer the known, or are happy to be players or experimenters in the about-to-be. "Bill Gates is the leader of the parade because he sees where the parade is going and gets in front of it," a person who did not want to be named told Stephen Manes and Paul Andrews. His critics say he does that through theft, bullying, and lies. Many believe that Bill's day is over—he no longer runs the company he founded, and Google has replaced Microsoft as the digital company everyone admires, envies, and fears. Could be, but then Bill has moved on to fighting malaria and AIDS and trying to transform American education, so maybe even in shifting from Microsoft to philanthropy he is being true to form: wrestling with the coming issue while the rest of us are stuck in the past. See what you think.

ONE

First Principle of Getting Rich Fast: Pick the Right Parents (or If You Can't, Learn to Be Intensely Competitive)

THIS IS SILLY—we can't pick our parents. But if you really want to know how rich people get richer, it's because many of them do start out with well-off parents. That does not necessarily mean the *richest* parents. Bill's great-grandfather had been a prospector in Alaska during the gold rush before opening a furniture store in Seattle. His son, the second Bill Gates, had to quit school in the eighth grade, because he was so exhausted from selling newspapers in the dark hours of the morning before school opened that he kept falling asleep at his desk. The third Bill Gates, his son, was the very first person in his family to graduate

Bill Gates the Third sitting with his father, who was Bill Gates the Third until he changed his name to Bill Gates, Jr. so that he would not sound like a rich kid (he wasn't) when he joined the army.

from college and went on to make his way as a smart, tough, hardworking lawyer. As another lawyer put it, Bill could be "a hard man, difficult and demanding." He showed his son by example how he had earned his success.

Mary, the mother of the Bill Gates this book is about, did come from wealth. James Maxwell, her grandfather, worked his way up from farm boy to banker in Lincoln, Nebraska. James went on to found the National City Bank in Seattle. His son and grandson were prominent citizens in Seattle, and accumulated enough money to leave a substantial inheritance to his family. Yet that was not the most important part of their legacy to the man who would eventually be the richest person in the world.

The Maxwell family used their wealth to become civic leaders, belonging to all of the most important charities and social organizations. That gave Mary a perfect opportunity. She flourished in doing charity work that brought her together with other leading lights of Seattle. Energetic, organized, and determined, she was the kind of can-do woman every board and committee was eager to find. Mary and her husband, Bill, were constantly volunteering: for the Children's Orthopedic Hospital; for the Junior League; for Planned Parenthood; for library campaigns; and, especially, for the United Way. Mary's "example," her husband recalls, "was stunning." That was not only true of her devotion to good work: she was comfortable with important people, and so passed on a sense of belonging and opportunity to her children.

Growing up in the Gates family gave Bill the confidence that if he did his very best, he could, and should, succeed. Yet there was a catch that came with this sense of assurance: the Gates family was intensely competitive. Bill was the fourth Bill Gates, but when his father, the third Bill Gates, went to serve during World War II, he did not want people to make fun of him—"the third" sounded as if he were some soft, privileged kid. So, he had officially changed his name from Bill Gates III to Bill Gates Jr. That left his son to be the "third." Adelle Maxwell, his grandmother, put it a different way, calling him "Trey"—as if he were a playing card.

Adelle (known in the family as Gam) loved cards. As soon as Bill was ready, she taught him bridge and kept telling him to "think smart, think smart!" Competing against his sister, Kristianne (who is four years older than he is), his parents, his grandmother, their guests—and much later Libby, the sister who was born nine years after he was—Bill was tested in every sort of game, from indoor card games to outdoor bouts of Capture the Flag. Very much like the Kennedy family—which is famous for its fierce touch-football games and quizzes around the dinner table, and which produced President John F. Kennedy, Senator Robert F. Kennedy, and Senator Edward M. Kennedy—the

TWO

Second Principle of Getting Rich Fast: Pick the Place (or Figure Out How to Make the Best of the Place Where You Happen to Live)

BEING BORN IN the right place can matter as much as being born to the right parents—and that was certainly true for Bill. Bill's family story—one ancestor a Yukon prospector, another a Midwestern farm boy who went West and made good—was a good part of the story of Seattle. Founded only in 1851, it was a city where people who had gone off to the Klondike, to the frontier, seeking to make new lives landed to settle down. A hundred years after it was born, Seattle had both the aura of calm success of an important city and the heritage of those who had struck out on their own and relied on their wits. It did not claim to be the biggest city, nor the wildest frontier. It was off to the north and west of most of the country but was pleased with itself.

After World War II, the city's economy centered on Boeing, the airplane manufacturer. So, in addition to Seattle's frontier and small/big city aspect, it was also filled with engineers. By the 1960s, the idea that you used science, math, sharp calculation, and clear planning to bridge from the known to the unknown was a big part of the spirit of the city, so much so that Seattle decided to hold a world's fair celebrating exactly that principle.

If you go to Seattle today, the most striking reminder of that 1962 World's Fair is the Space Needle: a clamshell-shaped structure raised some 520 feet off the ground and held in place by long, clean, steel beams that stretch up another 85 feet. The Needle was supposed to look a bit like a flying saucer while giving visitors great sight lines for viewing natural glories such as Puget Sound and Mount Rainier. That was a perfect summary of what Seattle wanted to say about itself: it looked ahead to the future, even the far future—from airplanes to space flight. Indeed, the entire theme of

the 1962 World's Fair was the twenty-first century—
then nearly forty years away. But at the same time, the
city was home to sailing, hiking, skiing, and camping
in the great outdoors.

Bill was seven at the time of the fair. It would be
the easiest thing to say that the exposition pointed
directly ahead to the man he would become, but he
has said that what he really enjoyed was going on fast
rides, not dreaming of what he would create in the
twenty-first century. And, to be fair, from 1889 when
Paris crowned its fair by opening the Eiffel Tower, to
1939 when New York's World's Fair called itself "The
World of Tomorrow," world's fairs have featured tall
buildings and predictions of the future. In that sense,
Seattle was just following along, doing its own version
of what others had pioneered. If you are looking for
predictions of Bill's future in this, Microsoft itself has
often been accused of selling itself as the leader in software innovation while actually trading on inventions
created by others. Nonetheless, the fair did devote a
lot of space to what exhibitors imagined would come
in the future.

The fair planners built a monorail—which

provided hours of fun for seven-year-olds but did not go on to replace trains and buses. They predicted that people would all soon be hovering in rocket belts and flying around the world in a matter of minutes—which is true only in video games and science-fiction novels. But IBM and the American Library Association each showed off what their computers could do. The Office of Tomorrow exhibit featured machines that could speak to each other and transmit letters. Two years earlier, Digital Equipment had announced the first computer with a monitor and a keyboard, available for just $120,000 (which would buy about as much as $816,000 today). But in Seattle, General Electric predicted that one day we would all have home computers so we could keep track of our expenses. Those who planned, built, and visited the Seattle World's Fair understood that computers would play an important part in the future, and that did matter.

Bill was born in a city of engineers, where the University of Washington was filling up with teachers and graduate students eager to master computing and sell their skills. He was born in a city that liked science. Indeed, the Science Exhibit at the World's Fair was

This poster for the 1962 Seattle World's Fair highlighted the monorail (which Bill enjoyed riding), the Space Needle (which still stands)—and the focus on the twenty-first century.

aimed at engaging young people and getting them interested in new research. He was born in a city ready to support the talented, especially if they were well-born, or at least well educated, and obviously bright.

Paul Allen grew up in Seattle, too. His family were Oakies much like the characters in *The Grapes of Wrath*. His grandfather was an Oklahoma farmer who had a terrible time in the 1930s. However, Paul's parents were outgoing, smart students determined to make the best of their skills. After high school they moved to California and then Seattle to pursue their education and start a family. While Bill was a product of Seattle's elite, Paul came from those rising with the city. Seattle had its troubles—poverty, racism, prostitution, even a history of labor strife. Yet Bill and Paul had the good fortune of being able to take advantage of the best the city had to offer: a school that could see the face of the future.

THREE

Third Principle of Getting Rich Fast: Get a Good Education

WHEN HE WAS in elementary school, Bill was easy to pick out: a small, skinny guy with a high, nasal voice who wore his clothes like an advertisement for being odd—his shirts buttoned up, his pants belted well above his waist. He would rock back and forth as he thought, his own rhythm and ideas mattering much more to him than how strange he seemed (this is still true, to this day). Maybe he was showing that he felt weird, or perhaps he did not notice how he looked— his thoughts were much more interesting to him than his appearance.

Bill would read the whole encyclopedia for fun,

excel at math drills, write a fourteen-page paper when a teacher expected two at the most. He could not understand people who didn't find thinking as interesting as he did, nor did he see why anything else mattered. When the family tried to hurry him along while taking a trip, he bristled at their impatience. "Don't *you* ever think," he'd demand. (There are several versions of this story, told by different family members. They all have the same punch line, but in some Bill comes across as more defiant, in others as more dazed, puzzled, and lost in his own world.)

Young for his class—he was born on October 28, just three days before the cutoff for his grade—Bill was still intensely competitive. In fourth grade, the kids had a ball game called Soak 'Em, where the aim was to hit other players, and he loved taking his shots. A geeky kid, younger than his classmates, who revels in showing that he is smart and doesn't mind giving, or taking, hard knocks is asking for trouble. Some bigger, tougher kid is sure to find him obnoxious and make him pay. A later classmate recalled feeling exactly that way. To him, Bill was "an extremely annoying person. He was very easy to sort of dislike. And

I think that probably me and a lot of people took a little extra pleasure in sort of bumping him while passing him in the hall and basically giving him a little bit of a hard time." Ignore the qualifiers "probably," "basically," and "a little bit," and you see an awkward, aggressive, unpopular kid who was getting banged around.

Bill's parents noticed another worrisome side of his school life: his desk was a mess; he didn't seem to pay attention in class; he was the kind of boy who laughs too loudly at inappropriate moments, a cutup who has his eyes on the boys he wants to impress—the crew he keeps trying to organize at recess—and not on demonstrating good study habits. As his father put it, his parents "thought he was trouble." Not only was Bill having conflicts in school, he and his mother were fighting all the time. Concerned, the family sent him to a therapist, but Bill used that as an opportunity to read up on psychology, matching wits with the man hired to help him.

How do you fit together the kid who reads through the encyclopedia and is lost in thought with the loud goof-off who clashes with his mother? Bill explained to one interviewer that part of his appearance of not caring, of being a bad student, was calculated:

> I remember girls always got so much better grades than boys, so it was wimpy to get good grades. So I only got good grades in reading and math. And they always had these things where they'd grade you on your ability and effort, so the goal was always to get an A3, which was the best grade with the worst effort. They'd give me like an A1, and I'd say "come on, I didn't try at all. This is bullshit, it's an A3, and I had a messy desk and everything."

Any way you slice it, Bill was both smart and trouble—which is what psychologists say is often true of gifted children. They don't quite fit in anywhere: able to think with adults but not be one, out of step with their classmates but wanting to be accepted. As the therapist told Bill's parents, they had a son who simply would never give in; you just could not beat him. Maybe Bill felt he had to play the part of the screw-up, even to the point of cursing at a teacher who gave him an A1. Perhaps juggling being smart and competitive with wanting to be liked was more than he could handle. He was either acting or acting out—or, most likely, both.

Growing up in Seattle gave Bill one way to resolve his conflicts—games, hikes, scouting: activity in the great outdoors. Every summer, Bill, his parents, and his two sisters vacationed alongside many other similar families in cabins out in nature. The place was called Cheerio, and the kids organized their own Cheerio Club, which evolved into a full-fledged Cheerio Olympics. The games were competitive, but in the spirit of nonstop fun: adults and kids were all jumping, running, hopping, and swimming together. Bill, his father recalled, liked water-skiing and other solo sports more than team games. And the boy who defeated a therapist and would not back down to his mother also famously set his own water-safety rules. But playing games was one way Bill could be both ferociously competitive and part of a family, a clan, a pack.

Scouting was a more organized version of outdoor hijinks, and it suited Bill perfectly. Indeed, Ann Winblad—a woman who knew him very well as an adult—

said that, at heart, Bill is a "12-year-old Boy Scout" who is always saying "'where's the adventure? Where are we hiking to? Where are we marching to? What happens next?'"

Scouting allowed Bill to be energetic and driven while being part of a group, but his parents were still worried. They were not confident that his outdoor fun would translate into better classroom experiences—and they were right. So after sixth grade, they decided to take him out of public school and put him in private school. That is where principles one, two, and three come together. The Gates family preferred public school, but when they saw a bright son who was troubled, they asked around, learned of the perfect private school, and had no trouble paying to send him there.

Paul Allen's parents were not well off, but they knew how much of a difference school had meant for them. Like Bill, Paul was bright but could not get interested in school. He would sit in the back of the classroom reading whatever books he liked, not paying any attention to the lessons. So his parents found a way to come up with the $5,000 a year (which is the same as about $26,000 today) it would cost to send him to the same private school as Bill.

The boy who recalled bumping Bill in the hallways actually met him in private school. He saw what would have happened to Bill in a different environment: "In public school the guy would've been killed."

At just the right moment, Bill's and Paul's families moved their sons to just the right school. Like a tugboat nudging a ship away from dangerous shoals and out into clear water, both sets of parents took their sons away from situations where their personalities would hurt them and put them into an environment where there were many bright, odd kids.

The boys were sent to a school with a firm code and yet with teachers who had the time and freedom to adapt to different learning styles. Maybe that is one reason why today Bill spends so much of his money on education—on developing new kinds of teaching that are attuned to individual students. He knows the crucial difference a school can make between a student who is floundering and one who is flourishing. Recently he confessed to a reporter that he likes going to YouTube to find lectures by physics professors. He sees the future of education in those free talks, saying that "if you're a motivated learner, and want to learn about any topic, geology, medicine, computer science . . . you can go and find it." As Bill discovered, the drive to find out what you want to know can lead you anywhere, and everywhere.

Lakeside School, the private school Bill entered in seventh grade and Paul in ninth, was a boys' school, as it would remain until Bill was a junior. Being a smart-mouthed young kid who was most at ease standing at the blackboard writing out algebra equations was not on the royal road to popularity. Indeed, his dad recalls that even as an upperclassman it took Bill two weeks of fretting before he asked a girl to the prom (if this is the same prom mentioned in *Gates*, she turned him down). But there were other kids like him—the sons of Seattle's professors, ministers, and lawyers who enjoyed being bright, sarcastic, and really quick with numbers. They were nerds.

No one knows exactly where the term *nerd* comes from. Dr. Seuss used it in 1950 in *If I Ran the Zoo* alongside a drawing of one of his hairy, grumpy, stern-eyed creatures. However, there are hints that the word dates back to a Canadian company whose engineers are rumored to have had N.E.R.D.—Northern Electric

Paul Allen (seated) and Bill Gates at Lakeside.

Research and Development—printed on plastic pocket protectors. A nerd, in other words, was grouchy and annoying (as in the Seuss book) but also odd, smart about abstract things such as numbers, and completely unaware of the latest fad or fashion. On a middle-grade and high-school popularity scale in 1967, when Bill came to Lakeside, the nerd sporting a plastic pocket protector was nestled on the bottom—the exact opposite of, say, a shaggy-headed guitar player in a rock band. But if you really look at what "nerd" implies, it is not entirely negative. For a nerd is hardworking and smart. He may not be cool, or a tough he-man, or suave, but he is completely at home with numbers and gadgets, and eager to put his ideas to the test. In Bill's second year at Lakeside, the school gave him and his fellow nerds the most spectacular present: a terminal linked to a computer.

Here again principles one, two, and three come together. Bill was at a school wise and wealthy enough to purchase access to a computer in 1968. At the time, cool kids all over the country insisted that they wanted to reject the whole modern world (except for electric guitars, records, and radios) and become a new kind of freedom-loving tribe. To them, computers stood for "the military-industrial establishment"—the government and big business crushing rebellious individuals. Sometime that year, on a boat off the coast of Florida, a group of San Francisco musicians wrote "Wooden Ships." The song imagined a world after a nuclear war, where the free people would reject radiation suits and metal, and would instead "ride the music." As sung by the Jefferson Airplane—true pioneers of San Francisco psychedelic music—and later by Crosby, Stills & Nash—whose harmonies were a highlight at Woodstock—the song stood as a kind of fantasy-quest promise for the hippie generation. Many other songs warned of California falling into the ocean and promised that Atlantis would soon rise again (both, apparently predicted by psychics). The Age of Aquarius, as another song from 1967 announced, was dawning, a time of "harmony and understanding," of "visions" and "revelation." (The song's title is "The Age of Aquarius" from the musical *Hair*, if you want to hear it.)

But at Lakeside it was different. The school's brainy outsiders could try out a computer for themselves—test-drive it, in effect. While masses of teenagers copied the tie-dyed look and hoped for revelations, in a Seattle private school, a very small set of teenagers really were blazing their own trails. They were scouts, and they had found the path that would lead them on their great adventure.

FOUR

Fourth Principle of Getting Rich Fast: Pick the Time (or Figure Out the Advantages You Have from Being Born When You Were)

EVEN LAKESIDE COULD not actually afford a computer. Instead they bought an ASR-33 teletype, which was linked to an outside computer. The computer Bill and Paul used most often was a DEC PDP-10 (a later version of the PDP introduced in 1960) by a phone line. First built in 1965, the ASR-33s looked like large typewriters that were fed by giant rolls of paper. They could receive information from the PDP or transmit code to it at the rate of ten characters (regular letters, numbers, or symbols) per second.

Today, computers are set up to make it easy for us. We type out instructions in English or click on a famil-

A teenaged Bill Gates finds another use for the phone line on the ASR.

iar icon that gives us a visual clue to what we are doing. But what we have now is the result of the computer revolution in which Bill played a key part. When he was growing up, nothing in a computer was designed for the ease and comfort of the user. Instead, if you wanted to take advantage of the power of the machines, you had to speak to them in their own language.

In very simple terms, a computer is a machine that knows one thing: the difference between "on" and "off"—or, if you put that in terms of numbers, between 1 and 0. The machine can figure that out very quickly; so if you string together a group of 1s and 0s (which is called "binary code"), the computer can now treat that set as a pattern. This is just like the dots and dashes of the Morse code used by telegraph operators. In the binary code used by most computers, it takes a string of eight 1s and 0s to spell out each familiar letter or number. For example, uppercase A is 01000001, while lowercase a is 01100001. So the ASR typically was sending ten strings consisting of eight 1s and 0s each second. By contrast, the high-speed Internet connections available in many homes, libraries, and schools today send thousands of characters each second, which is also why they can transmit sound, movies, audio, and pictures.

You could say, "Poor guys, they had to put up with an extremely noisy machine that was not even a stand-alone computer and could barely squeak out a line of type." Indeed, every simple calculator you have used is a far more advanced computer than the ASR, but that is precisely the point. The Lakesiders had the chance to learn about computing at just about the same time as the most advanced computer engineers in the country. Today when you start on a fast machine, someone else is in graduate school learning to build something you will see in five years. In computer engineering today, being young can be a disadvantage: you have to catch up to learn what others already know. In 1968, a young person interested in computers had an advantage. Bill and his friends were motivated, had time, and had a machine to play with. In a way it is like the events in the X Games versus those in the Olympics. Young people are inventing many of the moves that make it to TV—or at least they were just a few years ago. Athletes who train for the Olympics are surrounded by coaches with decades of experience. The Lakesiders were part of the generation who were the Tony Hawks of computing.

At four A.M. on May 1, 1964, two professors at Dartmouth College first ran Beginner's All-purpose Symbolic Instruction Code (BASIC). John Kemeny—a shy, one-time assistant to Albert Einstein—and Thomas Kurtz created this simplified language so that more students could make use of computers. Their language allowed students to write instructions that could actually get computers to do things, even if the young people were not programming wizards. No one had to pay anyone for a copy of BASIC; the professors made it available for all to use. Just four years later when the ASR arrived at Lakeside, the students had that accessible language waiting for them. The Lakesiders had a step up into computing, and they were learning this language not long after it was invented—perfect timing. A teacher who had lobbied for the computer and helped the kids get started on it reported that it took Bill just "a week to pass me."

The students had their computer and were learning fast, but computer time was expensive. It was not like now, when the computer you write on has enough memory to do just about everything you want it to do. The ASR was only useful so long as it was linked to the PDP. Still, Bill and his schoolmate computer pals Paul Allen and Ric Weiland (both tenth-graders) knew what a machine like this ought to be able to do, so they set out to do it. They worked out practical programs—such as one that turned letter-based grade-point averages into numbers—and fun things, such as a computer-based game of tic-tac-toe.

The attitude that Bill, Paul, and Ric had at the very start was the essence of what made them so successful.

They were not bothered by any limitations—their lack of experience and knowledge, the capacities of the machine, the time limits established by school. Most of us would complain, look around for someone to help us, or decide to put off computing until the machines were easier to use. They understood what should be possible, and they were going to make that happen. That confidence and determination took them a long, long way. To Lakeside's credit, when the teachers saw what their young men were doing, they encouraged them and got out of their way. The teachers did not mind that their students quickly surpassed them. Perhaps that attitude was related to Seattle being the city of engineers—a place of tinkerers and builders.

Being in Seattle helped the boys in another way. One of the Lakeside moms was a partner in a new firm named Computer Center Corporation. C-Cubed, as it was called, planned to make money by selling its services to Boeing—doing the crunching and processing for the airplane giant. But first C-Cubed needed to make sure its own computers were in top form. Who could they find to put a fancy, new, large computer through its paces? Who would be motivated enough to run programs

fact, he never finished, which is important—but not in the obvious way. He was not defeated; he was just less interested in the product than the process. He was out to take an idea, a concept in his mind, and make it real—whatever the skills he needed to learn, however much time it took. He gained by trying. In a way that is like the best of the computer games we have now: it doesn't matter if you fail to reach level 4 this time; what you learned can help you next time. But Bill and Paul and Ric were not playing games created by someone else; they were figuring out how to create games.

Today, we all know about computer-game addicts— kids who spend all of their time clicking away in alternate digital worlds. Bill was a computer addict before the term was known. Next to being on the computer, nothing mattered to him, certainly not how he looked or what he wore. So dirty laundry would pile up in his room and he'd just leave it there. The C-Cubed computer was near his house—by bus. But some evenings he'd sneak out and stay there so late that no buses were running, and he had to walk the couple of miles back home in the cold of the early morning.

Psychologists have spent a lot of time studying animals that are hooked up to machines that reward them for doing one task and punish them for doing another. A bird, for example, might get a food pellet for pecking one key and a slight shock for hitting another. The scientists watch to see how long it takes that bird to always go for the food and avoid the shock. In a way, the C-Cubed computer was like one of those experiments. Bill, Paul, Ric, and the other brainy outsiders of Lakeside were now linked to a machine that rewarded their interest, their intelligence, their determination. On it they could build new things, they could stretch their capacities, they could move out just a bit from the known to the possible. Like the birds in the experiments, they never wanted to stop; they just wanted more mind pellets, more chances to work with the machine.

The president of C-Cubed recalled that the teenagers were "fearless. They would attempt all kinds of things. They picked it up far faster than the ordinary working engineer would. They would say, 'What if? What if?'" As Bill and the others experimented, they impressed the adult programmers, who took them seri-

ously. "The novel thing," programmer Dick Gruen rec-
ollected, "was that we were treating high school students like real people." That was the fourth principle
in action—a young enthusiast was welcomed, not
treated as a gofer. The gap between university-trained
computer experts and eighth- to tenth-graders was not
too wide.

How thrilling—to be welcomed in a community
of experts, to be testing yourself, to find out if you
can make what you imagine real. However, there is a
danger when young people gain a sense of power, of
mastery, of being able to think with—even outsmart—
adults. They may also decide that normal rules do not
apply to them. That is especially true when they are
suddenly asked to pay for something they have been
getting for free.

The sad moment arrived when C-Cubed no
longer needed to keep testing its computers, and so
the Lakesiders had to start paying for access time.
Strangely enough, even though they were on the
computer as much as ever, when the monthly bill
arrived, the boys owed hardly anything. How come?
One of the Lakesiders had hacked into the files that

kept track of who owed what for using the C-Cubed computer. Paul, who might have done it, liked the pure challenge of it—they were not supposed to have access to those files, so of course they wanted to see them. But they did more than look; they found ways to use the computers without being charged. In other words, they cheated.

There is nothing unusual about teenagers bending rules—sneaking into events for which they are supposed to pay, passing themselves off as adults to get into a club, "borrowing" a credit card number or an ID. For the Lakesiders, that blurriness about regulations merged with both their hunger to be on the computer and a sense of invulnerability. They could beat the system, so why not do it?

C-Cubed did not mind so much—in effect, the students had performed another test, found a gap in the system. But Lakeside took the violation more seriously and insisted that its students stay off of the C-Cubed computers for three months—all of the summer of 1968. That was an apt punishment. Yet when the Lakesiders defrauded a company, they merely lost computer time. They were rapped on the knuckles, while kept within the embrace of their school.

That sense of invulnerability—the students feeling that they were so good, so clever, so determined, so able to get away with whatever they wanted that they deserved whatever they could scam—was not only directed against companies. They even began to hide from one another. Paul found a way around the summer ban on using C-Cubed accounts by working from a computer at the University of Washington, where his father was the associate director of the library. He neglected to tell Bill about his windfall, and Bill was furious when he found out. Then C-Cubed failed and sold off its assets. Bill, and his now best friend Kent Evans, bought some of its computer tapes, which held valuable programs. They did not tell anyone, even their pals Paul and Ric. However, Paul found out and was "really upset . . . because I thought we had been doing all this stuff as a communal project and nobody had tried to take stuff off the side or make money on the side. It was an all-for-one, one-for-all kind of thing."

Paul stole the tapes and played dumb until Bill and Kent admitted they had made the purchase and kept it a secret. The question of how much the Lakesiders were

friends—musketeers taking on the world together—
and how much they were individuals—out for themselves—would come up again. Indeed, it points to one
of the key character questions about Bill Gates: when
does a healthy—in fact, truly admirable—determination shade into being cold-blooded, even inhuman?
And there are those who feel Microsoft itself has had a
similar attitude: a sense that it is so good, so smart that
it ought to be able to play by its own rules.

As Bill remembers it, his newfound confidence, his
sense of power and trust in his intellect, gave him a
new way to handle his family conflicts. He told one
reporter that he stopped fighting with his mother and
stopped messing up in class because he had found a
cooler, riskier, but more thrilling way to rebel, to test
himself against the world. He claims that he set himself the challenge of getting straight As without studying, without taking a book home. That certainly did
become his strategy later on, in college. But Bill is a
storyteller. He loved acting in family skits and starring
in high-school plays. So whether he really was smart
enough to ace high school without cracking a book or
if that is just the kind of tall tale he now enjoys retail-

ing remains a mystery. One thing is clearly true: the computer gave Bill a focus and a direction. And Lakeside gave Bill and Paul access to computing.

What horizons are there for a teenager today? Where can he or she be taken seriously and make breakthroughs alongside adults? When Bill is asked this, he often talks about robots and robotics. In a cover story in *Scientific American*, for example, he explicitly said that the state of robotics research now reminds him very much of where computers were when he and Paul started out. He has also spoken about biology—especially genetics—and the crossing place of brain research and computer research. Indeed, he thinks that ultimately we may be able to create a machine that fully matches all human thoughts and feelings. But those are the fields that occur to him, an adult.

Looking at the same question slightly differently, it was teenagers who invented text messaging and embraced MySpace, Facebook, and other forms of social networking. Those are not frontiers of science, but they do open business opportunities that adults may be slower to grasp. Recognizing just this possibility, Microsoft recently spent $240 million to buy a stake in Facebook—a company created by nineteen-year-old Mark Zuckerberg.

Bill is the model of the teenager who grasped the future, but it will probably take a twenty-first-century teenager or college student to actually see what is coming next.

FIVE

Fifth Principle of Getting Rich Fast: Dream Big, Seize the Moment, Build a Business

"I AM GOING to make a million dollars by the time I am twenty," Bill announced one day at Lakeside, and he meant it. He and Kent, especially, could not wait to create a company, to build a business. Even as an eighth-grader, Kent's dad recalled, all his son could talk about was how to "make money, barrels of money." That is one difference between Bill and just about any other person in America who was entranced by computers at the time. Not only was he hell-bent on mastering programming, but he was like a prospector in the earliest days of a gold rush. He could almost taste what was coming—the fit between what computers should be able to do, what he and his friends were capable of making them do, and what companies would pay to have done. He wanted the money, the success, but his drive was larger than that—he did not just crave wealth; he absolutely had to build a company that would be part of the new computing world. He needed to start a business.

Lakeside itself gave him an opportunity. Kent, Ric, Bill, and Paul called themselves the Lakeside Programmers Group and looked for work. When Bill was a junior, the all-boys' school merged with St. Nichols, a girls' school. Both private schools prided themselves on the wide variety of classes available to their students, but they were spread out over two campuses. How could the administration work out schedules that suited so many needs? The obvious answer was to let a computer sort it all out. A middle-school teacher who was savvy about computing had handled Lakeside's scheduling, but he died in a plane crash just when the merger took place. So the school asked the Lakeside Programmers Group to take over. They were to be paid just over $4,000 (the equivalent of about $18,000 today), but they would have to work really hard to get it. Kent and Bill, the two would-be millionaires, could be found at all hours working on the computers, even sleeping overnight in classrooms. They had their first big job, and they were going to deliver it at any cost.

The cost was too high. In May 1972, Kent decided to take a class in mountaineering. Knowing that Kent was not athletic and was worn down from his endless hours working on the scheduling program, his father warned him not to go. But Kent insisted. In one of those terrible moments that is almost too tragic to believe, he slipped on a snowfield, crashed into rocks, and died.

How do you deal with the death of a friend, your closest friend, when you are in high school? Bill found an echo of his emotions in the John Knowles novel *A Separate Peace*—where a wonderful boy, the narrator's best friend, the star of the entire school, is killed. The book beautifully evokes what it is like to have a glorious friend, and to lose him—though in the book we finally learn that it is the narrator's jealousy and envy that were behind the accident. Whether Bill, who stayed up those nights next to Kent and knew better than anyone how exhausted he was, also felt responsible for his death is impossible to say. With Kent's death, he lost the person who was closest to him—a cross between a best friend and an imagined lifetime business partner. Perhaps that made Bill just one step more isolated in his quest for success.

Bill's next business project was a collaboration with Paul that never succeeded in making money, but like the war game he kept trying to program at C-Cubed, the effort was as important as the result. What they began to learn about computing later proved invaluable (see page 73). They gained equally useful experience another way. Bill was a senior in 1972, and just after Christmas vacation he and Paul were invited to work on an amazing project. The local energy company needed help on an immense job, so Bill, a kid who had to finagle his way out of going to high-school classes, and Paul, a sophomore at Washington State University, would be sitting next to extremely good adult programmers and working on high-end computers.

Bill was having a good year—he got six 800s on his college admissions exams (the math SAT and five achievement tests) and by spring was accepted with special recognition at Princeton, Yale, and Harvard. But knowing that he could have his pick of colleges was nothing compared to working on the energy project; it was "mind-blowing. It was like a dream come true!" He got to meet John Norton, an expert on programming, which was like getting an all-entry pass for a rock concert. "He was a god! He would take a piece of source code home, come back and just totally analyze the thing. Just a high IQ act."

Bill finally went back to Lakeside to finish his classes and accept Harvard's invitation. But then he, Paul, and Ric rushed back to work for the energy company again over the summer. Nothing, literally nothing, mattered to them now but the buzz of work and the company of the best programmers they had ever met. Time had no meaning—a day was as long as they could work before they crashed, caught a nap, and worked again. They competed with one another, Bill reported, "to see who could stay in the building like three days straight, four days straight. Some of the more prudish people would say 'go home and take a bath.'" While other teenagers were calling adults uptight if they didn't like Jimi Hendrix, free love, or LSD, Bill thought a prude was someone who wrinkled his nose at a programmer who saw no reason to bathe or change his clothes.

"We were," Bill added, "just hard-core, writing

code." *Hard-core* is a favorite word of his, and it is really interesting. In one way it implies irresistible toughness—a hard core, as in "hard-core convictions"—something so set, so established, it cannot change. But there is also a darker side to calling yourself "hard-core." Programmers such as Bill and his friends treated themselves as if they had no human feelings, as if they themselves were computers—machines designed to meet the needs of machines. In fact, Bill has said that ultimately computers will write code, and do it better than humans.

Bill liked being a pure brain in a driven, abused body. There is a real glint of pride in calling yourself "hard-core"—you are tough, ripped like a body builder, proud of how hard you drive yourself. You don't have an ounce of mental softness, of the need for human comforts. You are burnished bright by your labors. And because Bill found that work ethic natural, he later used it as the standard for his company. He would expect his employees to be just like him, hard-core.

The director of the computer lab at Harvard, who saw all too much of Bill that fall, described what it was like to be around him in his hard-core phase. Bill was "a hell of a good programmer," but he was also "a pain in the ass. . . . He's an obnoxious human being. . . . He'd put people down when it was not necessary." As often as not, Bill's put-downs centered on brains. Ever since he was a freshman at Lakeside, his favorite phrase had been "that's the stupidest thing I ever heard of." In class he would raise his hand and spell out in detail why he thought another student's ideas were stupid—not just wrong, but ridiculous. Bill judged everyone he met by standards that were as binary as computer code. If you were as smart, relentless, and driven as he was, you were a pal. If not, you were nothing.

Bill did not mind sounding arrogant, offensive, or contemptuous; he didn't care if he made another person feel humiliated. He didn't care about feelings at all; he cared about IQ, relentless hard work, and good code. However, once he was at Harvard, away from the energy company project, all of that drive needed a focus, a channel. He and Paul kept trying to make their first project work. Then, in December 1974, they read an article that changed their lives.

To understand this turning point we have to pause for a moment and look at the world of computing at the time. Back in 1962 at the Seattle World's Fair, people were predicting that computers would be part of daily home life. When Kent and Bill had talked about building a company, they'd dreamed of putting "a computer on every desk in America." They were hardly alone. From science-fiction fans to hobbyists to computer scientists, many people understood what computers would eventually be capable of doing. Indeed, in the San Francisco Bay area, the Age of Aquarius mood of expecting UFOs to land and human beings to leap forward to a future of telepathy and revelation was blending with computer research.

Douglas Engelbart created a lab at Stanford University designed to "augment" the powers of regular humans through computers. His experiments led him to invent the computer mouse, windowing, a form of computer network, and the kind of clicking from one document to another we all use today. He saw the computer as a tool for mind expansion and was figuring out how to make it work. Listening to a lecture of his may have inspired Gordon Moore to make a startling prediction: he said that every year scientists would be able to put twice as many transistors on a computer chip as the year before. In other words, the power of computers would double and double and double again, on into the future. He later changed the timetable to every two years; but nonetheless, this was a vision of the future in which the capabilities of computers would be accelerating at a dizzying pace. Moore made his prediction (which is now known as Moore's Law) in 1965, and he has since been proved right.

In the late 1960s, the computer rocket was about to take off, but there was one giant step missing—first someone had to build a computer that was small and cheap enough to be used in homes, schools, or offices. Computer fans debate which was the first small, cheap computer—the Kenbak-1 in 1971, the Micral (which was only available in France) in 1973, the SCELBI in 1974—but for the sake of easy comparison, there is the Honeywell that was introduced in 1969 and which cost $10,000 (the equivalent of about $55,000 today), so it was hardly an item that most families were ready to buy.

Then came the crucial problem: figuring out how to set up the computers so that people who were not techies, who did not feel comfortable with sophisticated computer languages, could use them. Someone would have to figure out how to modify programming languages designed for giant computers and then build them into small ones. Once that happened, the computer revolution would begin, because the machines would not only be small and inexpensive, they would actually be able to do, well, anything a clever programmer could think up.

Bill and Paul knew that the big change in computers was going to come. As Bill remembers, "From the very beginning, we wondered, 'What would it mean for DEC [Digital Equipment Corporation] once microcomputers were powerful and cheap enough? What would it mean for IBM?' To us, it seemed that they were screwed. We thought maybe they'd even be screwed tomorrow. We were saying, 'God, how come these guys aren't stunned? How come they're not just amazed and scared?'"

The article that Paul happened to notice on a newsstand in December 1974 "stunned" him and Bill; now they were running "scared." *Popular Electronics* announced that MITS, a company down in New Mexico that had gone from making toy rockets to cal-

The cover article that told Bill and Paul the personal computer revolution had begun.

culators, was now selling Altair 8800, "the world's first minicomputer kit." Here it was, the machine Paul and Bill knew was coming—the affordable home computer. This was their moment. It was as if you were a kid who lived for baseball, played every day in the park, knew you were good, and dreamed of getting into the big leagues. Then you noticed a bus with a big banner reading *Today Only, Major League Tryouts.* By the time you saw it, you could hear the motor starting up, could see the doors starting to close. Your whole life depended on getting on that bus.

After he made his prediction about the growth in computing power, Gordon Moore helped to found Intel Corporation, a company devoted to making those ever more powerful chips. The brains of the Altair was a new Intel chip, the 8080. Paul had noticed Intel two chips ago, at the 4004. The 4004 could not even store the binary code for the full alphabet, but just seeing that simple chip made his blood run cold. He was sure someone was going to figure out how to use it to run a small computer. In fact, a very bright man named Gary Kildall did figure out how to burn a new programming language on a chip. He, Bill, and Paul would cross paths at a crucial moment, but that was not to come for another five years. With the 8080, programming was not going to be an obscure experiment. The question was no longer *Could this chip be the key to personal computers?* but *Who would turn that key?*

On January 2, 1975—as soon as possible, but probably timed to arrive after the New Year's break—Bill and Paul wrote a letter to MITS claiming that they already had "available" a version of BASIC that could run on that chip. According to Ed Roberts, the head of MITS, that was just one of fifty pitches he got, all from programmers insisting that they had the language he needed. He phoned the number he saw on their letterhead, but no one was home. In their rush to reach MITS, Bill and Paul had used letterhead from their last project—with the home number of a colleague's mother. No one had voice mail at the time, so Ed couldn't leave word he'd called.

The silence from MITS must have been terrifying. It was like finally asking someone you really, really care about to go out on a date and getting no answer. Should they call, anyway? Who should call? What should they say? You get a sense of their mood from the solution they came up with: Gates, the better pitchman, would call but claim he was Paul. Not only was Paul older than Bill, he was also a large, bearded, teddy bear of a man while Bill still looked like an awkward, skinny teenager. They thought Paul would make a better impression if he got to go down to New Mexico. That is the kind of plan you come up with when you are frantic, fearing you will sound young, inexperienced, and like a couple of crazy college kids but knowing you must get the job. You have to give them credit, though, to have the guts to call and not keep waiting by the phone.

Bill and Paul were picturing MITS as a big, important computer company that was about to sweep the nation with its new product. Bill stumbled out a pitch and a request: they had the program—"Can we come out and talk to you?" Ed said sure, they could come down to Albuquerque, but the company wasn't quite ready to see them. Could they come next month?

Great, the silence was not a rejection. The door was open; they had a chance. There was just one problem— Gates and Allen did not have the language "available"; in fact, they did not have it at all. They had one month to deliver in person, on a roll of punched paper, language that existed only as a promise.

Microsoft has often been criticized for a kind of theft: hearing that a competitor is about to bring out some cool new software, Microsoft claims to have an even better version of the same product when it actually has little or nothing. The promised Microsoft version is delayed and delayed and delayed—the promises piling up—but in the meantime, no one buys the real, or more real, product from Microsoft's competitor. In a way, Bill and Paul did that at the very start when they said that their completely imaginary form of BASIC was "available." But there is another way to look at this pattern: from January 2, 1975, on, Bill and Paul understood what should be possible, what they must be able to create. They had the confidence to dream big, and to define as real something that was only a potential; they bet on their own skill, brains, and effort. Pro athletes play their games faster than anyone else because they silence their fear and trust their trained bodies. Bill and Paul silenced their fears and trusted their skilled brains. From 1975 on, they were the pros of the software game, and most everyone else was a step behind. They claimed possession of the possible—in the name of a company that came to be called Microsoft.

SIX

Sixth Principle of Getting Rich Fast: Get the Best Out of Every Deal (can be read as "Take Advantage of Opportunities," or "Be Ruthless, Cold, and Calculating, No Matter Who Gets Hurt")

WHEN BILL WAS in sixth grade, he wrote a paper in which he imagined running a company. "To avoid personal liabilities," the eleven-year-old explained, "I am going to incorporate." His lawyer father helped him with the assignment, but that does not mean Bill was simply reciting the legalese without understanding it. Indeed, he told one interviewer that his first ambition was to be a lawyer, and you can see that throughout his career. One of his greatest gifts is the ability to understand a contract.

A contract is a kind of binding ground plan. It lays out rules for what will happen. I agree to give you my six best Magic cards so long as they have at least the following powers; you agree to give me use of your Xbox for three hours. If I lose one of the cards before the trade, you have the right to pick a substitute. If your parents kick us outside while I'm playing, I get to come back for the remaining time another day. Fair and square—unless, of course, your best games only play on a Wii, so you are happily gaming while I'm stuck giving up great cards for time on an outdated machine. I might not think to make sure the contract spelled out which games I got to play. Bill would.

Bill has the best lawyer's ability to see beyond what the words say to what they imply. Just as he built a company around future products, he lays out contracts that corral a breathtaking share of future earnings.

Bill and Paul had a month to create a form of BASIC that would work on an 8080 chip. How could they do that? They didn't own an Altair kit, and if they ordered one, they would lose valuable time waiting—in fact, more time than they knew, since MITS was swamped and way behind on orders. But this is where their prior work paid off. For their last project, Paul had figured out that he could use big computers to simulate very small ones. He got the specs for the 8080 chip—which were publicly available—then went to a large mainframe and created a program that mimicked the way an 8080 chip would handle information. In effect, he had a working model of a computer chip running within another computer. Bill now could program for the working model, testing and learning as he went.

Paul was not taking classes anymore at Washington State, and Bill had found a job for him near Harvard. So Paul split his time between delivering on their promise and going to his day job. Bill juggled college classes (to the degree that he felt he absolutely needed to show up) with programming, playing endless games of poker, and taking the occasional nap. People who wandered into the Harvard computer lab would sometimes see a disheveled, grungy guy asleep, his dirty hair falling across a keyboard. Bill looked like an addict, a computer nut, a loser. But he was just the opposite. The only real life for him was in the code he was writing; there he was sharp, creative, and efficient. He was

Paul Allen and Bill Gates in the early days when Microsoft was a cross between a scout camp, a university, a fraternity, and an extremely successful business.

relentless, hard-core. So was Paul, in his own way.

Take the very last night—just before Paul was to leave to bring their program to Ed Roberts. Paul went to sleep. Bill stayed up, reviewing everything to make sure they had not made a mistake. That was Bill—the man determined to win, who would not forget to check a single detail. Double- and triple-checking his product was infinitely more important than such a silly thing as sleep. But the next day, Paul got on the plane to fly down to Texas. He performed his own mental checklist and suddenly realized that they had never written the simple program to load it on to the 8080. And while there were only fifty instructions, Allen had to write each one in binary code. So, sitting on an airplane, he wrote out the commands—with no resource books or machines to help him, using only his own deep knowledge of code. That was Paul—the builder who knew computers inside out and could speak their language.

Bill and Paul made a great team, and in just a month, they delivered on their promise. They had never actually tried out their code on a real Altair, but they were almost sure, or somewhat confident, or at least reasonably hopeful that when Paul got off the plane, it would work. But there was something they did not know. Paul expected to be met by the executives of a successful electronics giant. Instead, he saw a large man standing next to a pickup truck. That was Ed Roberts, and when he took Paul to the former sandwich shop next door to the massage parlor that was the headquarters of the company, Paul realized how wrong they had been. And Ed had some bad news: he needed another day to get a computer set up with enough memory to test their version of BASIC. Paul did not have enough money to cover staying at a hotel for even a single night. He had to lean on Ed to put it on his credit card.

Ed and Paul's meeting was like the first date of two teenagers who have known each other only by e-mail. Face-to-face, they both simultaneously have the sinking feeling that the other is not what they had imagined. But they are stuck together and have to make the best of it. When the computer was finally ready, Paul did his magic—using the instructions he had written on the plane to load the program on to the 8080 chip. If all went well, the computer kit that people could assemble at home would now have a language that would actually allow them to make it do things. Paul wrote: "print 2 + 2." The Altair obliged, spitting out "4." The program worked.

Ed was "dazzled"; even Paul was "stunned." What might be, what should be, what could be—was real. Ed was thrilled to see the code work. Paul was amazed at how fast the tiny machine was—much faster than the mainframe he had used to mimic the 8080 chip. The present was over; they were living in the future. But what would the future look like in the icy logic of a contract?

Bill and Paul took BASIC, a program that was available to all for free, adjusted it, and now were about to sell it. On January 1, just before they wrote to Ed, they carefully wrote up a contract covering Paul's use of the chip simulator on their previous project so that no one who had been part of that effort would have a claim on Paul's later work. Not only that. How was it that Paul was able to create the 8080 simulation? Bill let him use computers in the Harvard lab. The computers belonged to the university—Paul had no right to use them. Worse yet, he and Bill were there at all hours in order to create a product that they hoped to sell. They were adapting Dartmouth BASIC, a program that its creators gave away; carefully excluding former partners; and making use of property that was not theirs in order to create what they hoped would be the foundation of their fortunes. Indeed, when Harvard figured out what they were doing, Bill was brought before a special committee, where he had to explain himself. He thought there was a real chance he would be expelled from the school.

Harvard (much like Lakeside) chose only to slap Bill on the wrist and tighten its rules on computer access, but that is only a small part of the issue of public and private in the very early days of Bill and Paul's great adventure. From the first, there has been a strong voice in the computer world that believes "information wants to be free." They mean "free" in two ways. They believe that ideas have been hemmed in, really imprisoned, by old technologies such as handwriting and printing. "Free" means that ideas, creations, and inventions can now much more easily spread and be shared. Ever since 1960, Ted Nelson has been promoting a vision of Xanadu—a world of interlinked computers in which information is constantly being shared in every possible way. In other words, you could click from any word or image in a computer file to every other use of that word or image on all the linked computers in the world. Instead of reading a sentence from left to right, you could leave any word in it to journey wherever you wanted. To this day, Nelson is still seeking to make his vision a reality.

Computers, then, allow the world to be in touch. However, people who view computing this way also mean information should be without cost, for free. This is exactly how the Lakeside Programmers Group felt when they changed the C-Cubed accounts so that they did not have to pay for computer time. You could say it is the same as Bill letting Paul into the Harvard computer lab. Hardly any Harvard students were in there, the computers were idle; why not let a great programmer in? This is the same view as those who created Napster, to share music files; or Linux, an operating system that is freely available to all; or, for that matter, Wikipedia, the online encyclopedia whose content is created by its users.

To these pioneers of computer freedom, Bill is the villain of all villains. Not only did he build his company around making sure everyone paid for his products and prosecuting anyone who copied them, but his entire fortune began by using and then hoarding what was previously available to all. In this view, he is the devil himself, for instead of the future that was born when the Altair computer printed "4" being one of unlimited freedom, it quickly become one of private wealth and furious fights over rights. The crucial issue is the term *copyright*.

In very simple terms (people devote entire careers to legal cases involving just this issue), when you create something, anything, it belongs to you. If anyone else wants to use it, you can charge them for it. Since you can make money on what you create, you are likely to keep inventing new things. That is the basic idea of copyright. I write this book, and if enough people buy it, I'll be encouraged to write another.

But to many people in the computer world, copyright is an old idea from a previous era. In fact, they believe that charging money to use copyrighted material discourages invention. If I released this book online for free, they argue, I might well reach more readers than I get by my publisher selling it, and some of those people might want to buy a copy of the book. This is like getting demo versions of some games for free online but having to pay for the complete edition. My many online readers might go on to make their own additions or revisions to this text. It would spread out from me to the whole world.

In the computer world, where so many ideas are shared, what is mine and what belongs to all of us? The advocates of computer "freedom" have created a new form of "copyright" called "creative commons," which again encourages and allows sharing of images, ideas, music, and programs. Since 2006, chapters of Students for Free Culture have been springing up in colleges across America. Most students join because they want the right to share music files as freely as they want, so they see copyright laws as "digital feudalism." Some members are also devoted to larger causes, such as bringing the Internet to poor countries.

Bill Gates immediately began to speak out against what he called computer piracy—hackers. (The word *hacker* means something different to computer fans. They see it as someone who does neat things on a computer, without any implication that he is stealing, but the more common meaning is someone who breaks into systems where he does not belong.) The deal he and Paul made with MITS required every single person who bought a program to sign a form promising to keep the actual code a secret. Not only was this a headache for both the buyer and MITS, which was supposed to keep track of the forms, it was insulting. It treated every customer as a potential thief. On the other hand, from the very first moment MITS announced the new version of BASIC that could run on its computers, people were in fact doing their best to copy, to steal, Bill and Paul's code. So who was the villain here: Bill and Paul for trying to control their code or the computer mavericks who did not feel they should have to pay for it? Does "information" want to be "free"?

While the original Dartmouth BASIC was and is freely available to all, Bill and Paul modified it to work on the 8080 chip. Without their "hard-core" labors, the Altair could not have used the code. Indeed, many years later the two Dartmouth professors came out with their own better version to sell. Napster and other similar free file-sharing sites have been shut down by the law. Today, iPods and iTunes—when you do pay for music—are the way most people download music, and the music industry has its bloodhounds out to find those who don't play by the rules. Linux is wonderful—if you are already comfortable with computers. Wikipedia has terrific information, as well as pieces that have been shown to be false. From an author's perspective, I am happy with my book; I am not so sure I want it to mutate into many "fan" versions of itself.

The reality is that people do want to be paid for what they create, while they also enjoy the greater sharing that computers make possible. We want both ownership and freedom. Even if Bill did not exist, if someone else had modified BASIC and made their source code freely available, eventually some business would have grown up around selling software—and thus would have been diligent about protecting its copyrights.

The early days of personal computing were much like the early days of a nation. In a time of pioneers, where there are not that many new settlers in a territory, you see two trends. In one way, people are more equal: a girl who was brought up to marry whomever her father chooses may realize she is strong and capable and has the right to her own choices; a boy who was told to be silent and obedient in a city now helps feed and protect the whole family and comes to trust his own judgment. However, in frontier situations, settlers also sometimes make their own laws, which may include terrorizing native peoples, holding slaves, and beating their children. Indeed, the hackers who create and send viruses that invade our computers and the spammers who clutter our in-boxes, are great believers in "freedom." They enjoy feeling that they have the power to disrupt the mighty, to send ripples all around the world. Few of us would be eager to give them more power.

Bill was like the railroad that came in to the frontier town—soon there are schools and churches and truant officers, so kids have less independence, less free time, less voice in their families. But now there is also a marshal to walk the streets, so that rustlers and outlaws stay away. (Some, of course, see the railroad as the biggest thief of all, turning public lands to private profit—the very same accusation directed at Bill.)

This analysis of Bill is all very fair and balanced, but then there is a second contract to consider. Bill and Paul worked so hard and fast to get their code ready for Altair that they did not even have an agreement defining their own relationship. They weren't the Lakeside Programmers Group anymore, so they had to hammer out a deal. Two friends who had known each other for years had given their all to create an exciting new product. How should they divide up any income that came from it?

The most obvious answer is 50/50, but that is not how the deal read. Bill argued that he should get more. How did he make that case to Paul? Sometimes Gates remembers the story as being that Allen had a job and

Bill Gates in his office at Microsoft in 1984, after being featured in People *magazine.*

he didn't, when they were taking their first steps as a company—Paul was being paid while Bill wasn't. Sometimes the argument is set down as Bill being at Harvard while Paul was at Washington State, so Bill was giving up more by turning his full attention to their new deal. If you track their initial investments, Bill put $910 into the company while Paul added $606.

Paul never had any trouble speaking his mind to Bill—employees recall hearing them screaming at each other, going toe-to-toe like heavyweight boxers. At times Bill would win by sheer persistence—he would keep pushing his point of view like a dog gnawing on a bone until Paul seemed to tire of the fight and give in. However, Paul was smart enough to know that Bill used that tactic—in fact, he would beat Bill at chess precisely because he would weather Bill's all-out assaults. So if Paul signed the deal, he must have accepted it—he has never complained about it in public. Even the split itself is hard to track down; apparently it started out as 60/40, changed to 64/36, then eventually migrated back to 60/40. Bill has defended the deal by pointing to that last adjustment—a sign, he says, of his acknowledgment that "the original vision" for Microsoft was "something we shared."

Why does all this matter? By the time this book is printed, that split means that Gates will have earned some tens of billions of dollars more than Allen has. Allen is still fabulously rich, a multibillionaire. But what does it tell us—that once the astonishing success of Microsoft became clear and any tiny difference made by Allen's salary in 1975 had been completely washed away, Gates still insisted that he made more out of the business than his friend, his partner, the cofounder of the company?

Would Microsoft have been any less successful if,

once the company was taking off, Bill had torn up his deal with Paul and split their shares 50/50? No. Would Microsoft have been just as successful if Bill were the kind of guy who was willing to tear up an agreement in order to be fair to a friend rather than stick to the terms of the contract? Probably not. Bill's cold, clear-eyed attention to success over any personal attachment made Microsoft the giant it is. So perhaps it was really Paul who got the best out of the deal. He left the company decades before Bill did. Maybe he knew that with a larger stake, Bill would be all the more monomaniacal, driven to make Microsoft into a money machine. Paul got a smaller percentage in a more successful company.

A friendship may turn into a business, but a business is not a friendship. Bill knew that as clearly as a computer reads binary code. Indeed, Paul was not the only pal of Bill's who lost out. Monte Davidoff, a fellow Harvard student, did some key work on Bill and Paul's version of BASIC. He was paid, but at the tiny hourly rate they could afford at the time. Monte was not granted a share in the company he had helped to create. Indeed, for a long time, Bill did not even acknowledge Monte's contribution. This ability to make cold-hearted business decisions, the willingness to place the letter of a contract over any personal emotion, does not make Bill the most likable guy in America, but it is one crucial reason why he is among the richest.

There is one last contractual matter that came up in 1975. Ed and Paul recognized each other as soul mates. In fact, Ed offered the guy-who-couldn't-pay-for-his-hotel-room a job right on the spot—taking charge of developing software for MITS. This was a great position for Paul, working with a company of builders—guys who liked getting inside the guts of a machine and figuring out how to make it work. By summer, Bill came down to join them. However, he and Ed were a bad match. As Ed recalls, Gates was hard to deal with. "He assumed everyone was stupid." Still, Ed needed the two hotshots, so Paul and Bill worked for MITS while also setting up their own company, Microsoft.

Microsoft's deal with MITS was signed on July 23, 1975, just as Altair computers equipped with Microsoft's BASIC started to take off. Some two thousand Altair kits were sold that year, and by the end of 1976, MITS sold one out of every four personal computers in America. With its exclusive right to the use of Microsoft's language, MITS was in a good position to dominate the computer market—but there was a catch. The contract specified that MITS must also do its best to, in effect, rent versions of Microsoft's work to other companies. That would be like two teenagers inventing a new design that revolutionized skateboards. They might contact an existing company and give it the right to make the cool new boards, but only if that company also tried to license the technology to others. The teenagers would be relying on the power of the company to transform the entire world of skateboarding. If the company hoarded the new design and did not try to license it, the inventors might very well take the firm to court. That is just what happened with Paul and Bill.

Microsoft hired its first two employees, former Lakesiders Marc McDonald and Ric Weiland, so that it could develop new version of BASIC for the new chips that were becoming available. As long as Moore's Law was in effect, chips would keep getting increasingly more powerful, so programmers needed to scramble to develop ways to make use of them. MITS machines with updated Microsoft designs had the lead over everyone, and by 1976, Ed decided to listen to an offer from a bigger firm. He agreed to sell his company for $6 million worth of stock in the new buyer. However, the marriage of Microsoft and MITS was already in trouble.

MITS wanted people to buy its computer, so it was not eager for the Microsoft program to be made available to other computer manufacturers. For its part, Microsoft wanted to license its product to as many buyers as it could get. Bill enlisted the help of his father's law firm and managed to convince a court that MITS had not lived up to the contract. In just two years, MITS lost out. While Microsoft was hustling to sell versions of Basic to every new computer manufacturer, its first partner got no share of that income. Microsoft was on its own, and on its way.

If you sign a contract with Bill Gates and Microsoft, you had better read it carefully and fully understand its implications. Or you might end up with nothing.

SEVEN

A Pause Between Principles

READERS EAGER FOR a business how-to or a history of Microsoft have gotten most of the attention so far, and there is much more for them just ahead. However, since we are talking about one of the richest people in the world, a slight digression is in order. How, some may wonder, did Bill spend his money once it started to pour in? In the main he was frugal—even as a very young millionaire he would buy cheap airplane tickets, not go first class. In fact, he called any lavish spending "decadent"—which is just about the opposite of "hard-core"—and prided himself on knowing which bargain products were just as good as glamorous expensive ones. Within Microsoft he was reluctant to hire more employees even when they were sorely needed and the business was booming.

Bill behaved as if he were more scared of losing than eager to flaunt how he was winning, which is one key to his personality. No amount of success—and being the richest person in the world is as financially successful as you can be—ever quiets his sense that someone else, some big threat, is crashing through the woods after him and is about to catch up and wipe him out. Even though Bill knows he is very smart, hardworking, and determined, he keeps seeing his own shadow out of the corner of his eye; he feels that someone just like himself is going to catch something he missed and leave him in the dust. *Stunned* is a word he uses often to describe some threat he sees coming that no one else seems to have grasped. He is never complacent.

All along, though, there has been one exception in Bill's expense account, one place where money is no object: he loves to drive extremely fast, and owns cars that are so tuned for speed that it took a bill signed by the president of the United States to declare one of

A Porsche 959. Bill owns one of the few models made of this supercar.

them legal. The quest for speed began when Microsoft was in New Mexico, next to MITS. Bill bought a green Porsche 911—a sleek sports car whose engine sits in the rear, behind the driver, which makes the car hard to handle at high speeds. He is notoriously not a very good driver; still, he is said to have pushed the Porsche up to 121 miles an hour—as fast as he could get it to go. Bill would speed and get tickets—speed, spin out, and need to have his car towed; speed any chance he got.

In 1978, Bill and Paul decided to move Microsoft back near Seattle where they had grown up—to Bellevue, Washington. Bill began to buy cars. He owned a Mercedes 300D Diesel, which the authors of *Gates* call "the fastest slow car in the world"; then a Porsche 930 Turbo, which was originally designed as a street legal racing car and could go from 0 to 60 in 5.3 seconds; he picked up a Jaguar XJ6 for a while, then a Carrera Cabriolet 964 and a Ferrari 348. Now he has just two cars: a Porsche 911 convertible and a really special automobile, a Porsche 959. The 959 is what is called a "supercar," which means it is more advanced than any other similar car—only 268 of them were ever made. The 959 goes from 0 to 60 in 3.6 seconds, making the 930 look slow; and Bill is said to have reached 170 miles per hour in his—50 more than his old 911. However, the car did not match U.S. standards for fuel emissions or safety. Gates had to keep his in a warehouse until he managed to convince President Bill Clinton to sign a special bill making his car legal—and so now it is safely parked in his thirty-car home garage.

Bill works all of the time, so when can he use his fast cars? In the days when security at airports was not so tight, he would leave himself just enough time to race from the office to the airport parking lot and then dash to the gate. He wanted any excuse to get that rush, that taste for speed. In a way it was like his

EIGHT

Seuenth Principle of Getting Rich Fast:
Understand How to Sell Your Mousetrap

AS THE SAYING goes, if you build a better mousetrap, the world will beat a path to your door. From 1974 (when the Altair was announced) on, the computer industry was bursting with inventions: new chips, new machines, new programs, new applications, new games, new displays, new networks. Radio Shack came out with its line of TRS computers in 1977; by the following year, it had sold 100,000 of them. Indeed, sales of personal computers quadrupled, from 48,000 in 1977 to 200,000 the following year. MITS sold just 3,000 of those machines. In just one year it went from industry leader to antique.

In that heated environment of constant innovation, where last year's hit might be this year's has-been, a new formula for success was born. If you built a machine that developers, customers, and computer-store sales managers saw as dominant, they would take it as the standard. The question was not *Is it better?* but *Is it seen as the player, the force to be reckoned with?* The computer world was littered with inventions that were in fact better but that failed because the company building them was not clever, or tough, or slick enough. As Bill himself put it years later, "I know that we will have the reality of the software. We will technically be the best software. But if people don't believe it or people don't recognize it, it won't matter. While we're on the leading edge of technology, we also have to be creating the right perception about our products and our company, the right image." Bill and Microsoft were by far the best at understanding this new model, and so while mousetraps all around them rusted away, they came to dominate the computer world.

To Bill's critics, this is the big problem with Microsoft. Because it is so large, and such a bully, it forces people to accept the second-rate. Apple lovers say their computers did everything Windows did, only earlier and better. And they are right. Tech-heads point to CP/M—an operating system that was created before DOS and worked better. Right again. Those who know their history pine for the Alto, created by Xerox at its experimental Palo Alto Research Center (PARC), which could have given us the kind of computer displays we enjoy today a decade earlier. Absolutely true. We need to look at all of these. But in each case, the company that built the better mousetrap flubbed its chance to bring the world to its doors. Microsoft did not, and that is why Bill Gates is so rich.

Xerox PARC of the seventies was the Camelot of computing—the great kingdom where magic reigned. Some still wish that, like Arthur, Merlin, and the Knights of the Round Table, it would return to bring goodness and justice to all. Indeed, it was a wonderland of invention. One way to tell the story of that lost dreamland is through a man who worked there.

Károly Simonyi was born in Hungary when it was a poor country ruled by the Communists. He did not have access to a school like Lakeside, but his approach to the world had something in common with Bill's and

Paul's. As a boy, he could not even scrape together all of the parts for a complete Erector Set, but he decided to use what he had to build a car with a transmission. Not as you might think, for the fun of playing with it. He just enjoyed the challenge, the abstract problem of figuring out how to do it. That was just like Bill and the war game he tried to develop. When Károly became a teenager, his father, a professor, introduced him to a former student who worked with computers. Like the Lakesiders, he was taken seriously and given the chance to learn at an adult level. Indeed, Károly escaped from Hungary to Denmark because he managed to land a programming job there—while still a teenager with just a high-school education.

Simonyi (now known as Charles, the English version of Károly) left Denmark for California in 1967 to become a student at the University of California–Berkeley. Contacts he made there led him to join the team at Xerox PARC. Xerox, the company known today for its copiers, created the PARC in 1970 as a place to develop new ideas. By the time Simonyi got there in 1972, Alan Kay had a very big new idea: Dynabook. This would be a portable, hand-held computer—what

Charles, seated at the center, when he worked at Xerox PARC.

we would today call a laptop—designed to be used by children. As a person grew up, he or she would interact with the computer, learning from it and changing how it functioned. This was two years before the Altair, so very, very few people could even imagine a home desktop computer, much less a laptop that would last a lifetime.

If today someone suggested that every child should be given a satellite that would rocket into space as he or she grew up, send back data and respond to questions, almost everyone would say that it would be too expensive. Dynabook sounded just as implausible in 1972. But at PARC it was an interesting challenge. And while Kay was imagining a computer for young people, others were figuring out what a home personal computer—they called it Alto—should be. Simonyi and the other programmers set out to envision, and then invent, the tools that would be necessary to make computers useful to everyone.

At the time, computer monitors showed one style of type, and only in capital letters. Bravo, the program Simonyi helped to invent, not only led to all the typeface and styling choices we now have on our screens; it allowed people to see on the screen exactly what would be printed out on paper.

We take WYSIWYG—What You See Is What You Get—for granted today. But it was one of those great Xerox PARC inventions. When you still needed to solder an Altair together to use Microsoft's BASIC, friends and neighbors of the Xerox team were begging to come in to the lab so they could write up and print out PTA announcements. "These weren't lab hackers or hard-core hobbyists," Charles recalls, "they just wanted to do something. That's when I said to myself, 'Wow, this is serious stuff.'"

The PARC innovators made desktop publishing possible. One team went to study how book editors worked, then came back and invented cutting and pasting, the click-drag-drop that makes it so easy to revise a document. Then they created the kind of screen display we all use: GUI (Graphical User Interface, pronounced "gooey")—for example, icons to click on to start programs or open files, drop-down menus, and pointing devices such as a mouse. A visitor who used Alto in the late 1970s was getting to use computers in ways the rest of the world would not experience until the 1980s.

Yet today the Alto is a rarity owned only by collectors. Xerox did not understand what was going on at PARC. Over and over the PARC team suggested that the parent company turn the experimental Alto into a machine sold to the public. Every time, Xerox said no. In fact, it gave away most of the Altos it had, and its efforts to make an expensive, high-end version did not work out. The PARC team did come up with one invention that delighted Xerox: the laser printer.

The laser printer was a fine innovation and a perfect product for Xerox but hardly the new frontier in home computing. Charles was restless.

In 1980, more than 700,000 personal computers were sold worldwide, with sales in the U.S. alone nearing the $1 billion mark. Charles knew he was smart, and he wanted to be rich. He needed to be part of this boom. So he visited a former colleague and asked him who he should see, where he should look for work. He was given a list with three names: the man who had created VisiCalc, a popular program that allowed people to do number crunching and spreadsheets; Gary Kildall, the man who had figured out how to program the original 4004 chip; and Bill Gates.

Charles happened to meet Bill first, and his search was over. Xerox PARC was a wonderful place where brilliant, creative people thought a decade ahead and invented the next stage of the personal computer. They had built a much better mousetrap, and failed to do anything with it. Charles came to work with Bill at Microsoft, and they set out to make the company not only successful but dominant. To explain how they did that, we need to jump around a bit in time and look at the fate of two other better mousetraps.

The Open Garage Door: Two Stories
Lead Back to Charles and Bill

While Xerox fumbled its chance to profit from the innovations at PARC, there was another computer company that was much more sure-handed: Apple. Apple was headed by Steve Jobs and Steve Wozniak—a team as creative and bright as Bill and Paul. In fact, they had built a machine that Alan Kay at PARC thought was the very first commercial effort good enough to criticize. In 1979, Apple was invited to visit PARC. Jobs loved what he saw and struck a deal with Xerox: Xerox received stock in Apple; Apple got a chance to look under the hood of the PARC innovations. This swap meant that Apple users would be able to click on icons, while people using any other kind of computer had to write out commands for their computer to execute.

To Apple fans—and there are many—their computer was visual, intuitive, and sleek while everything else was clunky, old-fashioned, and dull. On January 22, 1984, the company aired an advertisement during the Super Bowl that cost them more than a million dollars to create and broadcast. It brave woman smashing the rule of evil Big Brother (a play on the book *1984*, by George Orwell). The ad announced that the Apple Macintosh, a new computer that made use of the graphic displays developed at PARC, was about to go on sale. Apple was the computer for free minds, for creative people, for those who refused to be ruled by corporations. Apple was the "wooden ship," the "Age of Aquarius" for the computer age.

To get a sense of how the Apple story played out, here are a few facts. In 1980, Radio Shack was the leading personal computer maker in America, with 20 percent of the market, followed by Apple's 17 percent; IBM had a tiny 1.9 percent of the total of 600,000 PCs sold that year. Though the PC market was growing, just 0.5 percent of all Americans felt the need to have a computer in the home. Ten years later, in 1990, fully a quarter of Americans owned PCs, and Apple was in a neck-and-neck race with IBM to dominate the market. But by 1995, when nearly 40 percent of Americans owned computers, Apple was in serious trouble. Why? Why did Apple lose out to IBM, the very image of the grim corporation in the 1984 commercial? For

Bill haters, this is another tale of how a second-rate bully could profit from intimidation and theft. (For Apple's recent comeback with the iPod, see page 148.)

The main reason for Apple's fall was Apple itself. IBM computers were much slower to develop the cool graphics and the point-and-click icons that Apple users loved. However, IBM did allow other companies to make clones—similar computers manufactured by rivals such as Compaq, Dell, and Gateway. This gave customers a wide range of ever-more-inexpensive choices. Apple refused to let anyone make copies or versions of its computers. As more and more people felt they needed to have a computer in their office, dorm, or home, most were willing to buy a cheaper model that was pretty good instead of a more expensive one that was cooler. Apple remained the choice of designers, of desktop publishers, and of people experimenting with multimedia, but as the PC became a necessity, IBMs and their clones became the standard and Apples the luxury options.

You can't blame Bill for Apple's business strategies. In fact, Microsoft developed programs especially for Apple, so Bill profited from its success. Indeed, he has said that Microsoft wanted Apple to show people what cool graphics could be because his company was betting on creating Windows to do the same for IBM computers. Bill understood that the key to making money in computers was software—the programs people used and that made computers run—and so he needed to make sure his company would lead that field. But here is where it gets tricky.

In 1983, Paul Allen was diagnosed with a form of cancer. It was treatable, but it meant he would be away from the company for a long time. In fact, after recovering, he chose not to return. (He later agreed to serve on the company's board of directors, but he has no part in developing new products.) Microsoft lost its technology star just as Apple first began to show what it could do. That same year, Microsoft announced that it was coming out with a program that would allow IBM-style computers to have great graphics, icons, and screens. Microsoft did not say this, but the graphics looked remarkably similar to Apple's. What exactly does "remarkably similar" mean? Apple thought it knew: Microsoft was stealing the "look and feel" that Apple had pioneered. In 1988, Apple took Microsoft to court, suing it for, in effect, theft. It took years, but Apple lost the case. How come?

One day Bill was talking with Steve Jobs of Apple—after all, the two companies were doing business, even while they were rivals. Jobs explained the mood at Apple, where Microsoft was seen as an evil enemy. "I can't get my people to trust your people. . . . If your big brother punched my big brother in the nose, people wouldn't say your big brother punched my big brother. They'd say the Gateses are beating up on the Jobses." Bill's answer is one of the most revealing things he ever said. "No Steve, I think it's more like we both have this rich neighbor named Xerox, and you broke in to steal the TV set, and you found out I'd been there first and you said, 'Hey, that's no fair! I wanted to steal the TV set!'" Bill was right. Xerox had developed the "look and feel" of modern computer programs before Apple. But his little story also shows the mood of the computer world and the tone of his company: they were like teenagers let loose in a world of rich neighbors with open garage doors. They were all thieves, and whoever was fastest, cleverest, toughest would get the most stuff. They might growl at each other over their swag, but none of them had clean hands. Still, ask any Apple fan and he or she feels gypped. To them Windows was just a bad copy, theft in all but name.

That accusation is bad enough, but Bill's critics think it is only half of his crime. Microsoft staged its first demonstration of what would become Windows (and was then known as Interface Manager) in 1983. *Staged* is precisely the right word, because the program was as "real" as the magic at a kid's birthday party. They had nothing to show, so they ran some programs on a screen in a way that made it seem as if they could have many different operations going on at the same time. All they had was the intention, somehow, someday, of being able to create a new operating system that would let IBM machines act like Apples. There is a perfect word for the kind of fake program Microsoft launched; it is called "vaporware": it is as real as a mirage and dissolves anytime you get near it.

Bill and Paul had told Ed Roberts that their version of BASIC was "available" when it did not exist. In a month, they created it. Now Microsoft announced that it had what would come to be called Windows when it had only vaporware. Windows did not come out in April 1984 as promised, nor in November. And when a version was finally released in July 1985, it was really a test run. Even at Microsoft they thought of that version as a placeholder while they did the "real work" in-house. Windows, which had been "demonstrated" in 1983, went on sale in a not terribly impressive version in November 1985. The first edition to begin to live up to its promise debuted in the fall of 1987.

Apple was better sooner but made a bad business decision. Microsoft was later and worse but great at selling itself. One made a better computer, the other a better company, which leads us, once again, to Gary Kildall.

Back in 1980, just as the Apple team was learning about the PARC software, IBM decided that it really ought to start making personal computers. However, there was one thing it needed. Microsoft and others had created programming languages that worked on the chips in small computers. Yet a computer also needs a second kind of program that, in effect, runs the machine. Using BASIC, you can get things done, such as adding 2 and 2 to get 4, as on that fateful day in Albuquerque. The computer itself, though, needs what is called an operating system. In simple terms, an OS tells the computer how to use its memory and power to get jobs done—which steps to take in what order.

If IBM was going to compete with the Altairs and the Apples and the whole alphabet soup of small computer manufacturers that were selling machines, it wanted to be sure it had a very good operating system. The company built its reputation on being reliable, solid—the obvious choice, not a fly-by-night start-up. The company learned that the operating system it needed already existed. CP/M had been created in 1977 by Gary Kildall, who now ran Digital Research, Inc. An IBM team flew out to California to sound out the company about a deal. Not just any deal, but a major agreement. For while nobody was buying IBM personal computers yet, the company was confident that with its size, power, and know-how, it would soon pass its rivals. Selling an operating system to IBM in 1980 would be like selling a product that Google decided to put on every one of its search pages today.

However, Gary was not in the office the day IBM

arrived, and his staff were either dismissive or perhaps just reluctant to sign the deal the computer giant offered. Their doubts about the deal loomed larger than the nearly limitless possibilities of being a key supplier to IBM. Bill did not share their fears and hesitations. The second he learned that Digital Research had said no, he notified IBM that Microsoft had just the thing. There was just one problem—Microsoft had nothing at all. But Paul knew of a tiny Seattle company that had experienced troubles with DR, so it had created its own operating system—similar to CP/M but different enough to be a new product. Bill scrambled to buy all the rights to use the program. As modified by Microsoft, that was MS-DOS, which when IBM and its clones did in fact take over, became the dominant operating system.

Gary had the better mousetrap; Bill was the much better businessman. Gary's system was real. Bill's was a promise. But Bill delivered.

By way of Apple and DOS, we have come back to the day in 1980 when Charles Simonyi met Bill. Charles did not know about IBM and DOS. He obviously could not know about Windows, which was years

NINE

Last Principle of Getting Rich Fast: "How Does This Help Microsoft?" (Focus, Focus, Focus)

WRITERS OFTEN TRY to get an interview with Bill—I did while working on this book but had no luck, which is true of most of us, except when Bill has a new product to push and wants the publicity. But reporter Gary Rivlin was extremely persistent. He honed down the questions he had for Bill, made it clear why Bill was the only person who could supply those answers, and then just would not take no for an answer. Finally, Bill's equally determined publicist—who guards him as faithfully as a bulldog—explained what she needed from Gary: "What you need to do is help me explain to Bill how talking to you is going to work to Microsoft's advantage. That's what he's going to ask me. 'How will doing this serve Microsoft's best interest? How will it help the cause of selling more Microsoft products?'" Gary never did meet Bill, but he was allowed to e-mail him directly to ask about that 60/40 split with Paul and received the answer about the "original vision" of Microsoft quoted earlier.

Bill made himself into a force to help his company grow and to sell more products. Everything he did served that end. That is what a company, even a nation, wants in its founder. Think of George Washington and America. Washington made himself into the symbol of the nation he was helping to create. In 1787, during the Constitutional Convention, a group of people who knew Washington well made a bet. Gouverneur Morris claimed he could walk up to him and chat, buddy to buddy. But Alexander Hamilton had been Washington's aide and knew him better. When Morris strode up, put his hand on Washington's shoulder, and said, "My dear General, I am very happy to see you look so well," Washington plucked off the hand, stepped back, and glared at his friend with a look that would freeze an ocean. He was not being mean or proud. Rather he needed to make clear that he was no longer a person; he was a role.

Bill Gates as the face of his company—here at the launch of Windows 95.

In the same way, Bill Gates became Microsoft. From answering an e-mail to having a conversation in a hallway, everything he did was aimed at making his company the absolute winner, the ruler of America's fastest-growing industry.

Within the company, there were no frills, no sympathy, and no excuses. If an employee disagreed with him, Bill would scream, insult, intimidate. One early Microsoft worker remembers it this way: "You know, like 'you stupid idiot. This is what I said. Just listen to what I say.'" Why was he so abusive? One possibility hearkens back to his family—where he knew he was smart, and knew that he could succeed, but was constantly being tested in mental and physical games. He may have developed a sense that in life you are either a smart winner or a dumb loser. When an employee seemed not to be great, Bill feared that his whole company would be dragged down into being terrible. His own fear of being tainted with failure meant he constantly needed to see signs that his employees matched his capacity for success.

This interpretation fits Bill's personal psychology, but there is another way to see his behavior: not as a personality trait but as a strategy. As Bob Wallace, one of his first employees, recalled, "He always wanted you to argue back. It wasn't personal. He would say, 'that's stupid!' or 'that's brain damaged!' . . . but it wasn't like you were stupid or brain damaged." While Bill told people to just obey him, he was actually testing them. He wanted to see who had the guts, the brains, and the quick wit to yell back. Those who challenged him and made him either change his mind or defend his positions were his favorites. His company was a shark tank where only those gifted with the highest intelli-

The 1992 Microgames – big business as a summer camp.

gence and the most unshakeable confidence could survive . . . and only so long as they were also willing to make work their entire lives. As Paul said, "We would just work until we dropped."

If Bill's abuse, his bluster, was really a gambit, that suited a company where games, puzzles, contests requiring employees to demonstrate their intelligence mattered a lot and went on all the time. Starting in 1986 when the event was just a barbeque with a band, Bill, his parents, and his two sisters organized the Microgames—a cross between the old Gates family contests and the Cheerio Olympics. There were physical tests, races on land or water, singing and acting—and then treasure hunts or other forms of puzzles where people needed to work out clues. The players could be Microsoft employees, friends of the Gateses, guests brought in to join the fun. While the events changed each year and could be as silly as anything counselors could dream up at a summer camp, the constant testing was an echo of what went on every day in the halls of the company. Ida Cole, Microsoft's first female vice president, described the company perfectly: "It was kids at camp without adult supervision."

As Microsoft grew, it had its pick of the best computer engineers from the top universities in America, and even the world. But the company did not look for people with doctorates in computer science. Instead, it wanted young minds, people who were really bright, would work without stopping, and could think in new ways—echoes of Bill and Paul and Charles. Often enough, a job interview would involve another game, another puzzle. The applicant would be asked how he or she would go about solving a question that had no obvious answer:—the point was not to "get it right" but to show clever and nimble ways of addressing problems he or she had never considered. For example, how would you figure out how many people die in Seattle every day, if you could not look it up?

Microsoft came up with a way of paying its employees that was itself a kind of game. It set its salary scale below that of other computer companies; employees took a pay cut to go to this fabulously successful firm. However, they were granted stock options—that is, if they stayed long enough (employees did not actually get stock until they had been with the company for a year or more). And if Microsoft ever made its stock available to the public and if that stock went up in value, employees could become really rich. Employees were betting their present against their future—the future they would help to create with their intelligence, determination, and endless hours of hard work.

Bill built a company as a giant game, with himself as the harsh, even cruel, puzzle master who just might also be a magician capable of turning your ideas and sweat into gold.

Then there was another Bill—the great salesman. When he wanted to make a deal, Bill became a different person. He was just as relentless, but with the strange ability to disarm even the brightest and most wary potential partner. Mitch Kapor, the designer of the popular spreadsheet program Lotus 1-2-3 and chairman of the nonprofit foundation responsible for the Mozilla browser, put it this way: "Competing with Bill Gates is like putting your head in a vise and turning the handle. He doesn't take no for an answer, and he keeps coming back." But Bill used more than force and persistence. Kapor also found himself bending to his "hypnotic will."

There is a moment in any argument, any negotiation, when most people are ready to stop—this has gone on too long, they say to themselves; life is too short. Bill would keep going, pushing for the other person to break. That is like his split of Microsoft shares with Paul: his goal was not to be liked, to be seen as a regular guy, but to take advantage of every opportunity and to build the most successful company. Bill has a scientist's clarity about what he wants to achieve, matched with a general's willpower. Neither of those traits requires emotional sensitivity, so even as he wins, he leaves behind bruises.

Bill the internal ringmaster and Bill the irresistible salesman are only two of the ways he became the company. Bill uses his star status in ways reminiscent of Donald Trump or, for that matter, Sean Combs. He is a person but, just as much, a personality, a brand.

When Gary Rivlin visited Microsoft, he noticed company calendars filled with photos of Bill, the company library stocked with magazines that featured him on the cover. Indeed, every time Microsoft was about to launch a new product and needed publicity, Bill was center stage. When Microsoft was just getting started, most computer buyers were hobbyists who eagerly read reviews and discussions in industry magazines. So Bill and Paul began cowriting a regular monthly column in *Personal Computing* magazine. That was one way Bill made sure every person interested in computing knew about him. He made equally good use of conventions—once-a-year gatherings of everyone who was anyone in computers. Bill would survey the floor, looking carefully to see what the competition was doing and making sure everyone was talking about Microsoft. He would give a rousing speech; he would appear in photo-ops; he would give interviews to all of the

The authors of the best biography of Bill Gates found the perfect quote about that convention. "You couldn't take a leak in Vegas," one person who was there recalled, "without seeing a Windows sticker." Microsoft's goal is always to dazzle, to overwhelm, to seem inevitable.

By 1986 it was easy to understand why Bill was selling himself and Microsoft so hard. The company was going to allow the public to purchase its stock. The more people who thought Microsoft would succeed, the more they would pay for the stock, and the more the millions of shares Bill owned would be worth. Microsoft had its first million-dollar-sales year in 1978, when Bill was twenty-three. When the company stock went public in 1986, the company was doing so well that he was immediately worth $233 million. The Microsoft employees who had taken the gamble and hoarded their stock options were millionaires, too. A year later, Bill was the youngest self-made billionaire in history, and by 1992 he was the richest man in America. Today he is among the richest people in the entire world.

Microsoft began the computer boom when Paul

met Ed and the BASIC program worked. The computer was no longer a fantasy machine, a monster used in labs, or a toy confined to the benches of the motivated hobbyist. As the world realized the potential of the personal computer, Apple and the IBM clones competed to be the dominant brand. Microsoft supplied the operating system IBM needed. Then, like a roulette player with a big stack of chips, Bill bet on both the red and the black, and cleaned up twice—when Apple took the lead and when PCs with Windows caught up and triumphed. By the late 1980s, as people had ever more powerful computers running Microsoft Windows, Microsoft set out to dominate every application: Microsoft Word in word processing, Excel in number-crunching and spreadsheets, Internet Explorer in networking, the Encarta encyclopedia on CD-ROM, and more. Under Bill's leadership, Microsoft rode, led, and then ruled the first twenty-five years of the computer boom. He changed the world.

TEN

Cracks

MICROSOFT ROSE TO dominance in the Wild West period of the computer world. As Bill had said to Steve Jobs, they were all teenage boys out to steal from their rich neighbors. And like teenage boys, sometimes they formed into packs, and sometimes they fought. In the 1980s, every year brought rumors of new alliances—a large company buying a smaller one that had made a hot product. However, some of these deals went sour, and every year also brought lawsuits as one company accused the other of stealing its inventions. Many of these cases were settled with agreements: when one side had a sense that it might lose, it would offer the other enough money to drop the case. The bigger Microsoft got, the more often it found itself in court. But the company has always been good about keeping large—and by now astronomical—reserves of cash. It always possessed as much money as it needed to buy off anyone it could not defeat in court. Yet there was a disturbing drumbeat in these cases—the scent of something unsavory. The word is *monopoly*.

In the game of Monopoly, we all want to win—to own hotels on the best squares, and then collect ever higher mounds of rent money. For that hour or so, we like being monopolists. But generally, "monopoly" has a bad ring; it brings up images of nineteenth-century robber barons gouging farmers as they gobbled up smaller railroad systems and set ruinous prices, or the miserly John D. Rockefeller's Standard Oil Company, which heroic trustbusters such as Teddy Roosevelt took on in court. From the moment Charles Simonyi and Bill looked ahead to the company's future, Microsoft aimed to dominate every aspect of personal computing. Another word for total domination is *monopoly*. As Microsoft seemed to be nearing its goal, the question was whether a new TR would try to stop them.

A monopoly is not in itself illegal. Let's say you invent, manufacture, and sell an antigravity device, and no one else knows how you created it. You will have a monopoly on antigravity; bully for you. Bill and his team felt that they were like that inventor; they were just smarter, more hardworking, and more determined, and so they built better programs and applications that people wanted. But going back to the analogy, if you build an antigravity device and make tons of money and then whenever a rival surfaces, you find a way to crush it, that is different. If you use your size and wealth to intimidate companies into favoring your product and rejecting those from upstart competitors, you have used your monopoly position to stifle competition. That hurts the public, because instead of getting to choose between products, instead of seeing newer, better, perhaps cheaper devices each year, they can only buy yours. You have gone from innovator to tyrant. In 1989, the Federal Trade Commission began looking into Microsoft to see if it was bending, or breaking, the rules.

The investigation was not public at first, but Bill haters were delighted since many of them were called in to give evidence. They knew something was cooking, but the FTC investigation dragged on for years without making any announcements. Finally, in 1993, the commission gave up; they could not decide whether or not Microsoft had broken the law. But later that year, the Department of Justice brought a new case, and this was precisely about whether Microsoft was abusing its position as a monopoly. While the company and the government came to an agreement in 1994, the Department of Justice was not satisfied, and in 1998 the DOJ and the attorneys general of twenty individual states insisted that Microsoft had abused its power.

This was really big: the government was challenging Microsoft just as the Sherman Antitrust Act of 1890 had brought down Standard Oil. In fact, several of the charges against Microsoft were based on that century-old act. Bill testified, but not in Washington; he was filmed in a Microsoft boardroom. Commentators found him evasive, seemingly struck with memory loss, and fencing with his questioners over the meaning of individual words. The outlook for Microsoft was dark, and turned positively bleak on April 3, 2000, when Judge Thomas Penfield Jackson gave his first judgment. Microsoft, he concluded, had been precisely the kind of monopoly the law was designed to prevent. In fact, it must be broken into two companies.

The courts can and have required just that when they feel a company is so large and so ruthless that its competitors have no chance. It is like a school in which two best friends keep causing trouble. A principal might split them up, put them in separate classes, and assign them mismatched schedules so they are never together. Microsoft's enemies were doubly thrilled; Bill's company would be cut down to size, and the ruling would prove that they had been right all along: Microsoft won by cheating.

Of course Microsoft appealed, and Judge Jackson himself was severely criticized for having given anti-Microsoft interviews to the press while judging the company. He, however, felt Microsoft's top managers had goaded him by their disregard for the law. Their testimony "proved, time and time again, to be inaccurate, misleading, evasive, and transparently false. . . . Microsoft is a company with an institutional disdain for both the truth and for rules of law that lesser entities must respect. It is also a company whose senior management is not averse to offering specious testimony to support spurious defenses to claims of its wrongdoing."

Judge Jackson's view of Microsoft was similar to that of Bill's longtime critics. Rob Glaser, who has left Microsoft, puts it this way: "In Bill's eyes, he's still a kid with a startup who's afraid he'll go out of business if he lets anyone compete." The same Gates trait that drove Bill to build Microsoft meant he would do anything to crush his competition. If you are inclined to see the company as dominated by a culture of bullying and greed, you have the words of this intelligent, thoughtful judge to use as proof. However, a careful observer might have noticed a clever strategy in the behavior of the Microsoft leaders: once they got the judge angry, they had grounds to object to his handling of the case. If the managers baited him and set out to get his goat in the hopes that a new judge would be more on their side, they were just using a smart legal tactic. Ever since he'd been at Lakeside, Bill was known for calling others "stupid" as much to test them as to insult them. In effect, the entire Microsoft team treated the judge as if it were Bill insulting an employee in a hallway. The judge fell for it.

On appeal, Judge Jackson was removed from the case, the company was allowed to remain in one piece, and the penalties against it were relatively mild. While you can find stern words about Microsoft on the legal record, in effect the company won. After more than ten years of government investigation, Microsoft was not only the leader in operating systems and applications, but its browser, Internet Explorer, was totally eclipsing its rival, Netscape. This was one of the central issues in the trial. Nearly all IBM-style computers were sold with Windows, and Windows came with Explorer, which was difficult or impossible to remove. Wasn't that an unfair advantage?

Microsoft's defense rested in part on a really interesting theory. The question is, when there are two products available to the public that do similar things, why does one win and the other lose? And why is that victory total—such that the loser often completely disappears?

The answer, according to one clever study, is what is called a "feedback loop." Once one choice is preferred by a few more people—and as Microsoft showed with its 1983 Windows launch in Las Vegas, advertising and promotion are as important as the actual difference between the products—the gap grows. If you visit a friend and see that he has a Wii player and not a Game Boy, you may want a Wii—to share stuff, to be as cool. Once more people are buying Wii players, a designer may decide to create a game to play only on that platform since he wants more users. Now more people have more choices on the one machine. A difference that was small at first grows larger and larger, until 90 percent of people buy one game platform and the other product shows up at garage sales. Once you are seen as dominant, you dominate. That is Microsoft's view of the world. But it does not quiet those who still claim Microsoft twists arms to gain those initial advantages.

Since it resolved its problems with the DOJ, Microsoft has lost, or been forced to settle, cases brought by rivals such as Sun, AOL (for Netscape), and Novell. The suits have a pattern: companies claimed that Microsoft used its dominance in selling Windows to favor its own other products, such as Internet Explorer, and to crowd out rivals, such as Netscape. Settling all these claims has cost the company nearly $6 billion. In 2004, a court that governs all of the European Union agreed with Microsoft's critics, and this view was upheld on appeal in 2007. In Europe, Microsoft stands convicted of being a monopoly that unfairly limited competition and has been fined $1.35 billion for its actions.

At the least, Microsoft is so driven to win that it has abused its position. One alert business reporter, though, pointed out that even at $6 billion in fines, Microsoft paid less on cases it lost than its annual budget for researching and creating new products. After all, the world of business is not a fantasy novel; a villain steals a magic spell that gives him great power and uses this vile strength to spread his blight across the kingdom until an unlikely hero with a good heart and magic sword rises to return the spell to its rightful owners—the suffering people. Or is it?

In the 1990s, Bill and his team at Microsoft were trying to figure out what the next big phase of the computer boom would be. First, people had bought home computers. Now they were more and more interested in networking—e-mailing, searching, shopping, getting information through their screens. At the time, people paid to belong to a company such as AOL,

CompuServe, Prodigy, or Microsoft's own MSN that provided the connectivity. Each service gave you access to a controlled online mall, a particular news feed, and a set of buying options. But the kind of people who had never agreed with Bill, those who believed that "information wants to be free," were concentrating their efforts on a different kind of connection: the wide open Internet.

The Net is not a thing, like the protective lattice of rope beneath a trapeze artist in a circus. Rather, it is a net*work*, a relationship among discrete networks. In fact, that is precisely what it was designed to be. In the 1960s, the U.S. Defense Department wanted to create a way for computers to remain in touch even if many of them were knocked out by, say, a nuclear bomb. In most communications systems there is a center, a hub. If that command-and-control post is destroyed, silence descends. ARPANET was designed to overcome that problem—computers would be linked to one another without any center. Information would be broken up into small "packets" of binary code that would flow in many pathways. If some terminals blinked out, the remaining computers could still communicate. Instead of a center with spokes radiating out like a wheel, this was a web in which any one node might be in touch with any other. In order for that to be possible, many different sorts of computers needed to be able to communicate with one another.

In 1968, when Bill and Paul were at Lakeside learning how to bang out code on the ASR, Douglas Engelbart revealed to a packed hall in San Francisco the work that was going on in his Stanford lab. His demonstration was so amazing, one person who saw it said that "it was like a UFO landing on the White House lawn." Engelbart created the very first system that allowed people to click from documents in one computer to those in another. He set up e-mail, and even split-screen video teleconferencing. If Xerox PARC was Camelot, this was time travel—a visit from the future. The only problem with Engelbart's amazing system is that it was designed for the networked computers within his lab. While he was a true pioneer with excellent connections at ARPA, he was also a go-it-his-own-way individualist. Instead of becoming the creator of the Internet, he turned into a kind of New Age guru. Global connections through computers were a vision in the hippie San Francisco of 1960s that became a reality in the sober Geneva, Switzerland, of the 1990s.

Tim Berners-Lee was an English computer-software consultant; he could figure out how to get computers to do things. In 1984, he went to work at CERN, the European Particle Physics Laboratory, in Geneva, where scientists smash particles into each other at extremely high energies in order to learn more about the smallest bits of matter and energy. CERN had scientists from all over the world. They needed ways to share information. By 1989, Tim invented the "World Wide Web"—the "www" you see in many Internet addresses. That is a way for documents on computers throughout the world to be linked, so that files on the network in one lab could be used anywhere on the globe.

On his helpful Web site, Tim explains his basic belief about computing: "If you can imagine a computer doing something, you can program a computer to do that." Indeed, his vision of the Web is extremely idealistic: "The Web is a tool for communicating. With the Web, you can find out what other people mean. You can find out where they are coming from. The Web can help people understand each other."

Right now, billions of people are using tools Tim invented. He chose not to make a cent from that. In the early 1990s, while the commercial services were fighting with one another to sign up subscribers, Tim and people like him offered something else: the endless Web.

Tim's invention began to spread just as Seattle became the capital of the rock-and-roll world. A generation of musicians born at the end of the 1960s were developing their own sound, recording on their own labels. Bands such as Pearl Jam, Soundgarden, Alice in Chains, and, most famously, Nirvana were the voices of outsiders who wanted to be pure, wanted to be themselves, did not want to be defined by the expectations and norms of the music industry. In 1991, Kurt Cobain was the outsider, the grungy kid who was battered, neglected, but found his own way. (You can play "Smells Like Teen Spirit" now.) The Gen-X music of Seattle was the voice of those who felt they had nothing in common with a cold, domineering, monopolistic corporation—such as Microsoft.

In their small record labels, their indie radio stations, their storefront clubs, the Seattle bands were making a space for those outside the mainstream. In a way, they were speaking for the generation that was beginning to discover the Internet—a place that was not yet owned, sold, controlled. Cobain, though, did make a deal with a major label, went on a world tour, and then, struggling with drug addiction, killed himself.

Microsoft had nothing in common with the kids hanging out in Seattle clubs. Instead, it faced a series of business decisions: Would people use the Internet, or would it be a tool only for experts? And if the Net did take off, how could anyone make money with it? According to a professor who studied Microsoft, Bill's company was slow to develop a winning Internet strategy because the team tackling that challenge was in their thirties—in other words, too old. The people who solved the problem of how to make money on the internet were a generation younger.

The story of Sergey Brin and Larry Page is Bill and Paul (and, for that matter, Charles) all over again. They perfectly illustrate principles three, four, and five. Sergey was born in Moscow in 1972; Larry was the son of a Michigan State computer-science professor, born a year earlier. They never knew a time before personal computers. When they met at Stanford University in 1995, the Internet was as new as, well, programming in BASIC had been in 1974. Being young was once again an advantage, because no one knew much more than they did about how to guide searches on the Net. Many different "search engines" were available, but none was the clear leader. Web surfers would have to go from one site to another, comparing results, to have the confidence that they had really gotten the information they wanted. By 1998, when they set up shop as Google, Sergey and Larry had created a better way of searching and a better model for making money on the Web.

You do not have to subscribe to Google, as you once needed to do to join AOL or CompuServe. Google does not sell applications, as Microsoft does. Instead, Google apparently gives you ever more of what you want, for free. Google finds words on the Net, it finds images, and now it provides e-mail, maps and directions, quotations of the day, even your astrological chart—all right there on your home page and for free. These services are so popular that companies such as AOL needed to stop charging people or they would have lost every one of their subscribers. How does Google manage to give away what used to cost money?

Google offers you access to the Web, which gives it knowledge about your search patterns that it can sell. Every person who uses Google trails a string behind, like Theseus spooling out Ariadne's thread as he ventured into the Labyrinth to fight the Minotaur. Google analyzes those tracks and can then sell advertising, sell knowledge, to companies that want to know how to reach buyers. That is not the only thing it can sell: if you search Google under, say, "music downloads" or "college prep" or "Bill Gates," you will find pages of listings. Two kinds of answers pop up. First come the "sponsored listings," which are placements paid for by companies, and in general, the higher up in the search, the more they cost. This means you need to be cautious in looking at the sponsored part of a search list because you are not necessarily seeing the best, or the most popular, results; you are seeing what someone has spent money to make sure you notice.

After the sponsored listings come a second set, whose order is determined by a Google formula that measures how often a page is used, and how many other pages link to it. For many searches, there are no sponsored listings at all; for example, if you search under the name of your school, no other school would pay to jump ahead of yours on that listing—why should it? Google has various ways of determining where a name comes up in a search. Figuring out Google's rules matters so much that companies hire experts whose only job is to make sure their product comes up first (or, certainly, high up on the first page) of any Google search. However, the company that knows most about its searches, and thus has the most information at its command, is of course Google.

Microsoft arose at the very beginning of the computer gold rush. Bill's goal—and his achievement—was to make order out of the boomtown mentality of those early years. His company set out to win by being the one brand everyone would go to first. In order to achieve that, he drove his employees as hard as he did himself, expecting them to work sixty-, seventy-, or eighty-hour weeks, doing whatever was necessary to get a job done. Encarta, the Microsoft encyclopedia, was an expression of that phase of the company. Bill bought up companies that owned photographs, which meant that he could illustrate his encyclopedia as lavishly as he wanted while other companies had to shell out high fees to him. Microsoft was selling millions of copies of Windows to computer manufacturers, so it could easily offer them (pressure them?) to include a copy of Encarta with every machine. It would seem that Encarta would be the dominant encyclopedia of the twenty-first century. But it is not. Instead, if there is a new encyclopedia that everyone uses, it is the Wikipedia, which is a direct result of the Berners-Lee model in which people openly share ideas, images, even sound and video clips.

Encarta was a move of one massive company to take over yet another market. Wikipedia is a snapshot of the collective intelligence and goodwill of all its contributors. Each approach has its pros and cons, but in the early twenty-first century, Microsoft's is the one that seems dated, old-fashioned.

Google was born a quarter of a century after Bill and Paul started out. It is the anti-Microsoft. Sergey and Larry have stressed that they want their company to do no evil. There is no yelling in the hallways; instead, they hired a gourmet chef to feed their employees. They provide a gym and a free on-site doctor and dentist. Microsoft charged money for its version of programs such as BASIC, which were originally free. Google gives away e-mail and search capacities that you once needed to buy. Google is the company for the age of the Net and what is now called Web 2.0 (the age of MySpace, Facebook, virtual spaces such as Second Life). Instead of setting itself up as the dominator, Google seems to be the voice of freedom. But is that really true?

Which is worse—Microsoft insisting that it wants to make money or Google offering free searches that some company has paid Google to work in its favor? The very appearance of being "good" can be an illusion more difficult to penetrate than Microsoft's evident will to win. For example, Google has set out to make libraries full of books available to search—a perfect example of the "information wants to be free" mentality and the direct opposite of Bill Gates, who has bought the rights to many of the most famous images in the world and charges for every use of them. However, authors and publishers have objected—they never agreed that their books should be available for online searching. Is Google helping create a connected world, or being its own sort of bully, forcing individual authors who have little clout to choose between being shut out of the search everyone uses or giving away their work?

In order to get a foothold in China, Google agreed to allow the government there to limit—really censor—searches. As a result, a person using Google in China to look for information critical of the government, for example, will not be able to find it. Any company would want to sell to the billion-plus people who live in China, but Google has set itself up as better than "any company."

If the "feedback loop" helped Microsoft, it has been equally good to Google, which is now as dominant in search engines as Microsoft is in operating systems. Indeed, when Google went public, Sergey and Larry became instant multibillionaires themselves. Is one monopoly better than another? The 2007 European Court ruling against Microsoft is very likely to be extended to other monopolies, with Google being a prime example. Google is the Microsoft of the twenty-first century. The two companies are more like successive generations of businesses then complete opposites.

In order to compete with Google, Microsoft negotiated with Yahoo, grew frustrated and attempted to take it over, then retreated and indicated it would look for new ways to blend the strengths of the two companies. This is typical of an older, established company—it may no longer be able to create the new products that dazzle customers, but it is so rich it can buy other firms and so continue to grow. Microsoft's old competitor Apple, though, has been an exception to this rule. With innovations such as the iPod and iPhone, it has staged a twenty-first-century comeback while Microsoft's versions of similar products have fizzled.

Even as Microsoft and Apple continue their long fight, and both fend off Google, new businesses are sure to rival all of them. Mark Zuckerberg of Facebook, for example, is a generation younger than Sergey and Larry. As long as Moore's Law remains true, computers will keep evolving so rapidly that someone probably needs to be born with one stage of them in order to envision the next. So, very likely, a person who was born around 2000, in the world of social networking, is just now getting the first inklings of the next billion-dollar business for his or her generation. But where does that leave Bill?

ELEVEN

Can We Fix It?

BILL IS A builder. He built computer programs. He built a company. He built the rules for an entire industry. He built a massive fortune. Then what? Most adults also think of building on a smaller scale: having a family. Bill knew that would come someday, but while he dated and had a long-term relationship with Ann Winblad, the woman who described him as an eternal Scout looking for the next adventure, Microsoft was his true family. He could not imagine himself as a dad, coming home, putting work out of his mind, and playing with a baby. But in the late 1980s, he began going out with Melinda French, a manager who had come to Microsoft in 1987. A year later, he bought land to build a house—perhaps a home for a family?

Not at first: the house, which cost more than $100 million, was built as a showplace for the Microsoft-enabled home of the future, as if Bill were living in one of the exhibits at the 1962 World's Fair. Rooms are designed to be customized to the preferences of guests: the lighting, color, and temperature adapt to their choices, which are encoded on a chip when they arrive. The chip remembers their selections the next time they visit and also has ways to figure out how to balance one guest's taste for red with another's for blue if both people are in the room together. Instead of paintings on walls, screens can show any of the hundreds of thousands of images Bill owns, as if guests were living inside of an encyclopedia or a Web search. In a way it is a house built for the marriage between Bill and his company, but by the time it was completed in 1997, Bill and Melinda were husband and wife.

Bill married the woman who would be his ideal partner, but not in building a company. Instead, to-gether they would carry on his mother's work. In 1993, Bill's mother was seriously ill, in fact dying, from can-cer. Much of Mary's life had been devoted to philan-

Bill Gates and Melinda French at a Seattle Sonics basketball game. This photo was taken in 1993, the year that Bill's mother urged him to use his great wealth to give back to the world.

thropy, to charity work. Apparently she wrote a letter to her son and the woman she hoped he would marry urging them to accept the responsibility of their great wealth—to give back to the world. Bill and Melinda were married on January 1, 1994, shortly before Mary died. Melinda also recalls 1993 as a crucial year, but in a different way. She traces the moment that would define much of their future to a trip to Africa in 1993. There she saw women walking endless miles to sell what little they had in order to provide for their families.

Why should that be? Why should they have so little while she would be living in a $100 million home? "Bill and I believe," she later told a newspaper reporter, "one life is worth no more or less than any other."

Bill and Melinda did start a family—they now have three children—which Bill found more enjoyable than he expected. Melinda, it is said, also humanized their showplace home. In 2000 they set up the Bill & Melinda Gates Foundation. The foundation is the focus of the next phase of Bill's life, for in 2008 he plans to limit his role at Microsoft and devote his brains, his energy, his will, and his ability to reach anyone in the world to the foundation.

Bill started out by giving over $100 million to the foundation, and then increased the endowment to more than $2 billion. His money alone made the foundation the largest philanthropic organization in the world; and that is only part of its endowment, because Bill had become friends with Warren Buffett, an investor who is also always on the list of wealthiest Americans. In 2006 Buffett announced that he was giving away most of his billions to the Gates Foundation, with the special provision that the $1 to $2 billion that he'd give each year be matched by other funds and spent that year. At a stroke, the annual budget of the Gates Foundation doubled.

What can smart people do to help the world if they have billions to give away? The Gates Foundation has focused on disease in Africa, especially malaria and AIDS. In his typically blunt way, Bill points out that the world press is filled with headlines whenever a disease threatens a rich country, but deaths from malaria have doubled in the past twenty years and we hardly ever hear about it. The foundation is sponsoring new research on how to combat the disease, and there are early signs that a new vaccine that can protect children as young as one year old may be working. That in itself would be a great accomplishment, but Bill has done more than pay for research; he also uses his skill as a businessman in speaking to drug companies. Knowing that they could make much more money by developing expensive drugs that only help wealthy people, he argues that figuring out how to create a malaria vaccine would give a company knowledge it could later use in more profitable ways. Rather than trying to shame companies, he appeals to their own long-term goals. Very likely he is making the only kind of pitch he would have listened to while leading Microsoft.

In America, the foundation concentrates on education. Melinda has said that "everyone agrees that the failure of our high schools is tragic. . . . But we act as if it can't be helped. It can be helped. We designed these high schools; we can redesign them." Foundation money has made it possible for cities around the country to break up large high schools into smaller magnet and charter schools. The goal is to have a city filled with Lakesides, so that the future Gateses and Allens can find high-tech devices, and dancers can have stages, and student diplomats can visit the United Nations.

It is not clear yet that breaking up schools actually helps students; one early study suggests just the opposite. Just as he did with the early versions of Windows, Bill learns how to fix a product by trying it out, testing it, until he gets it right. That may not be much consolation to a student in a chaotic magnet school, but over the long haul, Bill's determination to make schools better is far more significant than the success or failure of any one plan. Bill and Melinda have also been active supporters of historically black colleges and of libraries.

The foundation has already had an impact beyond its specific grants, and that is reflected in Buffett's be-

Bill meets Nelson Mandela. The Gates Foundation has focused attention on diseases such as malaria that devastate Africa and are all too often ignored by the media and large drug companies.

quest. Bill is the model of the modern business success. When he put so much money and energy behind giving back to the world, it was a kind of challenge to other extremely wealthy people. Just as he created the model for how to build a company, he now demonstrated how a billionaire should behave. If his home set a standard for how to be lavish, the foundation is the best example of how to be gracious and humane.

How can we piece together the man whose business has been ruled a monopoly by the courts, who undercut his friends in deals and ignored the work of early collaborators; who was known for humiliating his employees; who has been called a thief, a bully, a liar, and worse by his rivals and who is accused of having stolen and hoarded what should have been free and shared, with the man who is doing more than anyone else on the planet to improve health care and education for those who need it most?

Here is one place where history can really help us. Andrew Carnegie was born in 1835 in Scotland to parents who were cloth weavers. While they did well for a while, they lost everything just as he was growing up, and the family moved to America just to survive. In other words, he was at the opposite end of the scale from Bill. But there are similarities. Andrew went to work at age thirteen, quickly moving from a twelve-hour-a-day job in a dark factory to running about Allegheny City, Pennsylvania (now part of Pittsburgh), as a telegraph messenger boy. The telegraph is the grandfather of the Internet—another system of communication that could go from node to node without a center. When a telegraph line was set up linking the U.S. to a station in Halifax, Nova Scotia (where Atlantic Ocean steamships stopped), Carnegie got the job of being the first Pittsburgh telegraph operator to take down the international news and messages. He was young, hardworking, and smart, and was there just as a new technology took hold. Sound familiar?

As it happened, another technology was also starting its boom, and creating opportunities for young men: the railroad. In 1852, when he was twenty-nine, Thomas Scott was made the supervisor of the new western division of the Pennsylvania Railroad. Scott hired the seventeen-year-old Carnegie to be the telegraph operator for the new line. The young Carnegie soon became a supervisor, and he was as tough on himself and his employees as Gates would later be. Carnegie linked the telegraph to his home so he could be on call twenty-four hours a day—hard-core. In his autobiography he admits he "overworked" the people who reported to him, and while he probably did not call employees "stupid," when a train was in a minor accident, he had one worker fired and two suspended without pay.

Carnegie, Scott, and J. Edgar Thomson—the man who hired Scott—built their fortunes together. At the time, it was perfectly legal for men who ran one company to give inside information to their friends. So, for example, a railroad company could buy its steel from a firm the railroad managers secretly owned; the railroad would overpay, and the managers would collect twice—from the profits of the railroad and from the inflated steel. Similarly, knowing where the railroad's tracks were to go, the managers could buy land, then sell it off at higher prices to those eager to have businesses near train stations. The trio used the formula of collusion and inside knowledge over and over again, making fortunes in oil (in the 1860s, the first oil wells in America were being dug right near them, in Pennsylvania), railroads, telegraph lines, steel, sleeping cars for trains, and steel bridges for trains to cross, then selling stocks and bonds in all of the companies they created and managed. In the railroad boom that followed the Civil War, Carnegie, Scott, and Thomson were making money just about as rapidly as, well, Gates would in the Internet boom about a century later.

Carnegie was getting so rich so fast, he could no longer see the point in it. He liked being a salesman, he liked writing articles about his work and his travels and being featured on the cover of a magazine, he liked the challenge of each new deal; but he had more money than he could ever use. When he was thirty-three years old, and worth the equivalent of about $75 million today, Carnegie wrote a note to himself about his future. He thought it was wrong to keep chasing after money, but he also knew that "whatever I engage in I must push inordinately," so he needed a new goal. Sitting at his desk in the St. Nicholas Hotel in New York City, Carnegie resolved that as long as he could provide for his mother and his home, he would spend his wealth "for benevolent purposes."

Carnegie did not actually follow his plan right away. In fact, he kept "amassing wealth" until he was, some historians estimate, the richest man in the world. In doing so, he often made promises that he knew were false or, at best, unrealistic. You could say he sold "vaporbridges"—crossings that were being built, but when they would finally be up, and how profitable they would actually be, was anybody's guess. Carnegie ran afoul of even the lax laws of the time and was taken to court on charges of making secret deals and covering them up. The charges were true, but the courts sided with him.

Carnegie was a much more outgoing, personable

man than Gates; he liked people, worked as little as he could once he got rich, loved art and culture, and lit up a room when he walked into it. His engaging personality made others like him, even when they disagreed. Bill's cold, off-putting bluntness makes people dislike him, even if they admire him. Still, Carnegie the businessman was like Gates the company builder: he enjoyed working with smart people and did not feel threatened by them. He loved organizing games, singing, and acting in shows. He was a brilliant publicist, strategist, and salesman. He made his real fortune by investing in a new technology—in his case Bessemer steel—and eventually creating a steel monopoly just when the nation needed steel. And he played very close to the line between legal and illegal. He followed his own rules and let any damages be worked out by lawyers and settlements.

But in the end he did just what he said. In 1889, he published a book in which he said that rich people in effect only gathered wealth, which they then needed to use for the good of all. He had already begun sponsoring the building of public libraries, first in Scotland, then America. Indeed, to this day you can find the "Carnegie libraries" he helped build throughout the country. When he realized he could not sponsor enough libraries before he died to give away his entire fortune, he created a foundation to carry on his work after he died. Carnegie believed that his business success and his philanthropy fit together; it was all just the way evolution works: those who are more skilled, more ambitious, accumulate wealth. They build companies. That is good because it creates new jobs and makes new products and services available to the public. As the companies grow, their smart founders get richer and richer. Then they use their wealth to help humanity. The more really rich people a country creates the better for everyone.

Perhaps Gates in his fifties was similar to Carnegie at thirty-three: a man who enjoyed his work but no longer saw the point in simply making more money. Indeed, when Gates speaks about Microsoft, it sounds similar to Carnegie talking about the good millionaires bring to society. The steel baron of the 1800s shows us that Bill's shift from cold businessman to generous patron is not so unusual. Indeed, many notorious tycoons are eager to pay for museums, hospitals, scientific research centers so that they are remembered as much for their donations as for their schemes and conquests.

But what was it in Bill's own particular mind and motivations that created such a big change in his life?

In a way, it was too easy. Once you are the richest person in the world, what financial goal would you set for yourself? Is staying number one enough of a test? Like Carnegie, Gates may want the challenge of using his mind, his fierce determination, his vast wealth "for benevolent purposes."

Gates has said that *The Economist*, a well-written and intelligent English journal, is his favorite magazine. In an article on the Gates Foundation, the magazine pointed out how difficult it is for a charity to really improve the world, how easily foundations can waste money without accomplishing anything. It could be that this is precisely why Gates is focusing on philanthropy—just as he had set out to get As without studying, promised to deliver programs he did not have, even drove too fast when he was not a good driver; he likes being on that edge where he might triumph or could completely crash and burn. If it was easy, why would he bother?

John D. Rockefeller became fabulously rich at the same time as Carnegie and, famously, created a monopoly in oil. In fact, it was his Standard Oil Company the government eventually challenged in court. Rockefeller, too, was a philanthropist, though in his case, he started giving away money at the very start of his rise in business. A devout Baptist, he saw charity as a part of his moral responsibility. Gates is a rationalist who has not the slightest interest in religion, so in that way he is completely different from Rockefeller. However, the old man was very careful how he managed the money he gave away: he pioneered gifts that got a group started but that they needed to match with their own efforts. His grandson David Rockefeller has been an adviser to Gates, who uses similar business models to make sure that his money serves to assist people who will be spurred to further efforts. If Carnegie gave Gates the model of the two kinds of success, the Rockefeller family has given him a vision of how to make the best use of the money he gives away.

History and psychology give us some insight into Gates, but then there is the nature of computers themselves. Programmers—such as Bill and Paul were in the beginning—work by themselves, for long hours, taxing their brains to figure out how to make a machine do what it ought to be able to do. This is solitary labor that calls for intelligence and willpower. It can encourage that computer-geek mind-set in which you are harsh with other people and value only brains and work—"hard-core," as Bill called it. But the result of all that work is the possibility of making new connections. Malaria in Africa may be more real to Bill because he has been to that continent, but also because he lives in a world of constant information flows: he is accustomed to seeing someplace far away as part of his world, linked by a screen. It makes sense that a man who built his fortune around putting the whole world in touch would then feel a responsibility to improve lives throughout the planet.

Paul Allen has used his Microsoft billions in ways that reflect his own interests: creating one museum dedicated to Jimi Hendrix and another to science fiction, buying the Seattle Seahawks and the Portland Trail Blazers, contributing to the University of Washington and to many charities in his home city.

It may be, then, that Bill and his "information wants to be free" critics have more in common than they realize. They argue that had Bill not grabbed hold of and then monopolized the personal-computer industry, software and creativity would have spread far and wide. However, if you look at his whole life, first the rise of Microsoft and then the foundation, in the end he probably will have done something of what they wanted. Yes, he accumulated great wealth; but then he has targeted that money for use spreading ideas, knowledge, information. Would more people in the world have benefited if Bill and Paul's BASIC had been given away? Would we be better off if gurus and visionaries gave us our software instead of monopoly-minded companies? Probably not.

There are, though, darker ways of seeing Bill's plans to focus on the foundation. Perhaps he is jumping ship. Bill may feel Microsoft is going to slide, and he doesn't want to be there for that. He may be so determined to win that he prefers to leave the company before it is visibly in trouble and instead wants to polish his image as a do-gooder. That way he leaves a legacy as a double winner: the businessman and the philanthropist. Microsoft is in the hands of Steve Ballmer, a friend and colleague of Bill's since college. Is Bill leaving a friend to fail? That would be as cold as his split with Paul, and not out of character. Or does he recognize that a younger, hungrier team is needed, that his time is over—whether he likes it or not? Or could it be that he knows Microsoft's image needs to be softened, so he is as much a poster boy for the company when he holds a hungry child on the cover of a national magazine as he was when he pitched Windows? All of these motivations are plausible. But does that matter? He is still giving away billions and billions of dollars.

Bill Gates created, conquered, and gave shape to the dominant industry of the last quarter of the twentieth century and is now working to improve the world of the twenty-first century. He screamed at his employees and has not been interested in being likable except when that serves his own or his company's interests. The company he molded in his own image has frequently been in trouble with the law. Writers have speculated that his combination of high intelligence, physical quirks—rocking as he speaks—and brutality to others suggest that he may have a disease called Asperger's syndrome—a mild version of autism. Maybe. But none of us is perfect. None of us is without edges to our personalities. He harnessed his most destructive energies and changed the world, for the better. That is more—much more—than most of us can say.

GLOSSARY

ALGOL ALGOrithmic Language was first developed in 1958 by an international committee; it was designed to work on any computer.

ARPANET ARPA—the Advanced Research Projects Agency of the U.S. Department of Defense—created a **network** in which computers could exchange information in a new way. Instead of a single line carrying a whole message as your voice is carried over a land line on telephones, now information would travel in "packets." That is, the parts of one message could be transmitted through many different routes. A **network** of linked computers could transmit messages without there being any one center. This new way of sharing information launched on November 21, 1969, and was the foundation of the modern **Internet**.

ASR Automatic Send and Receive. This machine had a keyboard and was connected by a telephone line to a large computer. In other words, it was not a computer itself, but provided a way for people to link up to, and make use of, the capacities of a large computer.

BASIC Beginner's All-purpose Symbolic Instruction Code. A **computer language** designed to enable users to give instructions to a computer even if they could not write out commands in **binary code** or did not know highly technical computer languages. This was a "higher level" language. That is, what the user wrote, sent to the computer, and got back looked more like regular English, but the computer was able to "translate" the commands into **binary** strings.

BINARY CODE Binary numbers have only two elements, ones and zeroes. For example, there is no numeral for 2; what we write as 2 is written as 10. Binary code strings together binary numbers in series. A computer can recognize the difference between on and off, so it can "read" strings of binary numbers. The PDP-10 that Bill used at Lakeside happened to use strings of six digits, not eight as was more common.

CHIP (OR MICROCHIP) The major change in computers, from being ever larger room-sized machines in the 1940s and '50s to the astronomically more powerful yet light and tiny laptops of today, was made possible because of the shift from vacuum tubes, to **transistors**, to integrated circuits on microchips. A computer needs a way to recognize two states, on and off. Vacuum tubes are like glass lightbulbs that have been set up so they can make an electrical signal stronger, and can also switch on or off. Many vacuum tubes together could allow a machine to keep track of many ons and offs. But they were bulky and hot—so not only did they take up space themselves, they required large air conditioners.

In 1947 three scientists at Bell Labs discovered that transistors—tiny circuits that were cheap to manufacture—could accomplish the same things as vacuum tubes, only they were faster and more reliable, so that one transistor could do the work of forty tubes. This made possible a new generation of somewhat smaller computers, starting with Control Data's CDC1604.

In 1965, two scientists independently discovered that at first thousands, later millions, of transistors could be packed together on a single chip made of silicon. These chips made the personal computer revolution possible.

COBAL Common Business Oriented Language was a **computer programming language** first developed in 1959. It was designed to be useful for businesses in, for example, keeping track of their payrolls. In modified forms, it is still used today.

COMPILER A program that takes in all of the **source code** that is being fed into a computer and then, once it has all of that information, translates it into terms the computer can use. This translated form is often called object code. An alternative means of translating source code is an **interpreter**.

CODE (OR SOURCE CODE) A programmer will write a set of statements or instructions for a computer in a form he or she can read; these then must be fed into the computer in a form the computer understands. What the programmer writes is called source code. This code is put into a form the computer can handle through the use of a **compiler** or **interpreter**. The version used by the computer is called object code.

COMPUTER PROGRAMMING LANGUAGE Computers cannot understand standard words as we speak and write them. Initially, instructions for computers were written directly in the **binary code** the machines could read. "Higher level" languages allowed programmers to write instructions in terms that were more similar to standard phrases—such as "print," "add," or "exit."

FORTRAN Developed in 1957, Formula Translation was a **programming language** that, among other traits, was designed to make it possible to translate complex mathematical expressions into much simpler forms.

GUI Graphical User Interface, pronounced "gooey." Typically, when we use computers today, we click on icons, pull down menus, drop and drag files, change fonts in an instant. These actions make our screens very much like physical spaces that we rearrange by hand. Until the early 1970s, computers did not function this way. To get a computer to do something, you had to write a command, an instruction, defining what it should do. Charles Simonyi and others at Xerox PARC developed this visual, or graphical, way of treating files. GUI makes computers much easier to use, since in most cases you don't need to know or look up specialized terms; instead you learn a few simple techniques that can be used on any machine. A child who can't read can still click—which is why there are many computer games designed for preschoolers.

HACKER In common usage, a person who hacks, or breaks into, a computer or network. In that sense, a hacker is like a thief, pirate, or spy. But for computer fans, the term just implies someone who does neat things on a computer—with no implication of breaking the law.

HYPERTEXT When I write down words, I hope they express what I wanted to say. That is text as it used to be known.

Because we now write on computers that can be linked to each other, we have a new kind of writing. With hypertext, I can embed links into what I set down, so that a reader can click through to another site, to more text, images, or sound, and it may also be possible for the reader to add to what I've written.

ICON Before the computer age, this was a visual image that inspired worship or devotion. Now it means any image on a screen that identifies files or programs.

INTERNET A **network** of computer networks. Even in the 1960s, a school or business might have set up their computers so they could speak to each other, and users could share files. Linking those separate networks to others throughout the world established what we now call the Internet. See also **World Wide Web**.

INTERPRETER A program that translates **source code** one command at a time, without creating any **object code**. An interpreter works with source code, translating it as it arrives.

MOORE'S LAW A prediction made by Gordon Moore that the power of computers would double every year. While estimates of the time frame have changed—two years is now commonly used, though some claim that is shrinking—the basic observation has proven accurate. Moore based his insight on the idea that the number of **transistors** scientists could put on chips would keep doubling.

NETWORK An interconnected chain, web, or set of linkages. As in a spiderweb, a network can hold together even if part of it is damaged, which is different from connections that all run through a central point.

OBJECT CODE Statements or instructions for a computer that the machine has translated into a form it can read, see **Code.**

OPERATING SYSTEM A program that tells a computer how to allocate its resources to accomplish its tasks.

PDP Initials for Digital Equipment Corporation (DEC)'s Programmed Data Processor. Bill worked on a PDP-8, then a PDP-10, linked to the ASR at Lakeside.

SIMULATION While trying to create the computer program for **Traf-O-Data,** Paul realized that he could learn how the chip they planned to use would function by creating a kind of model of it within a large computer on the Washington State University system. That way he could master the capacities of a chip he did not even have yet. This process is called simulation. When he and Bill rushed to create a form of **BASIC** that could work on the 8080 chip in the Altair, they adapted that same modeling process.

TIMESHARE Bill and the Lakesiders were able to work on the **PDP** in part because of a relatively new development in computing. Until the late 1950s, you had to come to the machine and feed data into it directly. But then clever programmers figured out how to have computers juggle many tasks at once, which was called timesharing. That allowed even students who were typing on an **ASR** far from the main computer to send commands and get back responses relatively quickly.

TRAF-O-DATA On page 60 I mention the business Bill and Paul created after Kent died. This was their plan to create a program that would make it easy for cities to count cars passing through a given point, and thus collect data on traffic patterns. The company found a few clients but was not a success. Working on this project was the first time Paul simulated a chip within a mainframe, and that knowledge proved invaluable to him later on.

TRANSISTOR Materials such as silicon and germanium have the property that, depending on their temperature, they can either pass or block an electric charge. In 1947 John Bardeen, Walter H. Brattain, and William Shockley figured out how to make use of these properties to create small, inexpensive circuits, or transistors, that could amplify electrical charges and do the work of vacuum tubes (see **chip**).

WORLD WIDE WEB As invented by Tim Berners-Lee, this is the system of documents linked from one computer to another all over the world.

WYSIWG What You See Is What You Get, a feature of **GUI**— what you create on the screen is what you will see when you print it out.

The Altair 8800: you had to solder it together by hand, and it could not do much, but this computer is the ancestor of the PCs found all over the world today.

NOTES

RESEARCHING BILL GATES was an interesting challenge for me, because he is the first living person I have written a book about. Had I set out to write this book in the 1980s, it would have looked different—then he was the triumphant, but hated, head of Microsoft, the face behind the Internet boom. The many articles, interviews, and Internet comments on him were either from fans who had made money with the rise of personal computers or from rivals and detractors who detested him. He was either the hero of American business or the devil who stole computing and made it a pale, poor copy of what it should have been.

Two key books about Gates—*Hard Drive*, by James Wallace and Jim Erickson, and *Gates*, by Stephen Manes and Paul Andrews—came out one right after the other, in 1992 and 1993, and reflected how Gates was seen at the time. Both books used as their resources extensive interviews with people who know, or knew, Gates, as well as magazine articles written during his rise. *Hard Drive* is more critical of him; *Gates*, while it exposed as myths many stories Gates told that were then repeated as fact by reporters, is more balanced. I think students will find *Gates*, in particular, to be a rich resource to consult but are likely to find the level of year-by-year, product-by-product detail more than they need to know. And much has happened to change, or perhaps sharpen, our image of Bill since the early nineties.

Courts have ruled that the animosity of his rivals had some basis, some real grounding. Yet Gates has completely changed his public role. He is not the monopolist but the philanthropist. I feel that writing now, after the fates of the largest suits against Microsoft, after the rise of Google and now Facebook, and after Gates has shifted his main focus from Microsoft to his foundation, means there is enough of an arc to his life to be able to talk about him in a measured, thoughtful way. Writing about Gates is also a way of writing about the computer revolution, a subject that has been studied and written about quite well.

My research strategy was to use *Gates* and *Hard Drive* as a base, spread out to other sources to investigate the history of computing and to learn more about the people in Bill's life, and then to use the Internet to find recent articles about Microsoft today in responsible newspapers and magazines. One of the most enjoyable sidelights in this research was learning about Douglas Engelbart and the way in which the hippie San Francisco of the sixties overlapped with the computer revolution, also being spearheaded in the Bay area.

I am grateful to Stephen Manes, who answered my questions and got me started on my research, and to Dr. Stross, who pointed me to a helpful article; to Pam Kruger and Dave Rosenzweig, who used their expertise in business journalism and computing to guide me; to Todd Bishop, a reporter at the *Seattle Post Intelligencer* who follows Microsoft, for insightful comments on the entire manuscript; to Emily Doyon and Emily LaVerrire of Portland, Maine, for proving to me, yet again, that teenagers are breathtakingly smart and articulate; and to Susan Schmitz and the eleventh-grade English class of the Notre Dame School in Quincy, Illinois, for making the reading and analysis of a draft of this book a class project, and teaching me a lot. Thanks, too, to Regina Hayes for giving me the chance to write this book; and as only she knows, precisely the one thread in the first draft she didn't like was the one that puzzled my teenage readers. I was so pleased to be able to tell them I had already made those cuts. Without the insights of you experts, and the engaged eyes of you teenagers, I would be truly lost. But, as ever, the mistakes here are entirely my own; none of these helpful people are responsible for any of them.

INTRODUCTION

"Bill Gates is . . .": Manes and Andrews, *Gates*, 296.

CHAPTER ONE

Second Bill Gates falling asleep at school: Bock, "Principled & Pragmatic."

"a hard man . . .": Wallace and Erickson, *Hard Drive*, 15.

"example was stunning": Bock, "Principled & Pragmatic."

"think smart . . .": Manes and Andrews, *Gates*, 18.

"winning mattered": Isaacson, "In Search of the Real Bill Gates."
For the Kennedy family, see my *Up Close: Robert F. Kennedy*.

CHAPTER TWO

For a useful chronology of the history of personal computers, see
http://www.islandnet.com/~kpolsson/comphist/

CHAPTER THREE

"Don't *you* ever . . .": Manes and Andrews, *Gates*, 16.

"an extremely annoying . . .": Manes and Andrews, *Gates*, 34.

"thought he was trouble": Manes and Andrews, *Gates*, 24.

"I remember girls . . .": Manes and Andrews, *Gates*, 18.

"12-year-old Boy Scout . . . next?'": Manes and Andrews, *Gates*,
22.

"In public school . . .": Manes and Andrews, *Gates*, 34.

"if you're a motivated . . .": Michael Singer, InformationWeek's
Microsoft Weblog. "Bill Gates . . . YouTube Watcher, Zillow
User." May 9, 2007. For different theories on the origin of the
word "nerd," http://home.comcast.net/~brons/NerdCorner/
nerd.html.

You can find the full lyrics to either song by typing the titles in to
any search engine.

CHAPTER FOUR

"a week to . . .": Manes and Andrews, *Gates*, 27.

"fearless. They would . . ." and "The novel thing . . .": Manes and Andrews, *Gates*, 32.

"really upset . . .": Manes and Andrews, *Gates*, 41.

For Bill's story of how he decided to get As without working, see Walter Isaacson, *Time*, "In Search of the Real Bill Gates," October 20, 2005. Manes and Andrews point out many instances in which Bill's stories—especially about his childhood and teenage accomplishments—were exaggerated.

CHAPTER FIVE

"I am going to . . .": Manes and Andrews, *Gates*, 46.

"make money . . .": Laura Rich, *The Accidental Zillionaire*, 13.

"mind-blowing . . ." and "He was a god! . . .": Manes and Andrews, *Gates*, 54.

"to see who . . ." and "We were just . . .": Manes and Andrews, *Gates*, 56.

"a hell of . . .": Manes and Andrews, *Gates*, 58.

"that's the stupidest . . .": Manes and Andrews, *Gates*, 34.

"a computer on . . .": Laura Rich, *The Accidental Zillionaire*, 13.

"augment": John Markoff, *What the Dormouse Said*, 4.

"From the very . . .": Laura Rich, *The Accidental Zillionaire*, 18.

"the world's first . . .": Laura Rich, *The Accidental Zillionaire*, 25.

"available": Manes and Andrews, *Gates*, 70.

"Can we come . . .": Manes and Andrews, *Gates*, 71.

CHAPTER SIX

"To avoid personal . . .": Manes and Andrews, *Gates*, 20.

"dazzled" and "stunned": Wallace and Erickson, *Hard Drive*, 80.

The Electronic Frontier Foundation is the leading advocate for the "information wants to be free" idea. See http://www.eff.org/ for more information.

"digital feudalism": Rachel Aviv, "File-sharing Students Fight Copyright Constraints," *The New York Times*, October 10, 2007.

"the original vision . . .": Rivlin, "My Five Minutes with Bill Gates."

"He assumed everyone . . .": Laura Rich, *The Accidental Zillionaire*, 33.

CHAPTER SEVEN

"decadent" as a favorite term for Gates: Manes and Andrews, *Gates*, 235.

"the fastest slow . . .": Manes and Andrews, *Gates*, 180.

For more on "supercars," see Marc Aronson and HP Newquist, *For Boys Only*, 10–11; for the Porsche 959, use any search engine to look it up.

CHAPTER EIGHT

"I know that . . .": Manes and Andrews, *Gates*, 238.

"These weren't labs . . .": Lohr, *Go To*, 128.

"I can't get . . .": Manes and Andrews, *Gates*, 225.

CHAPTER NINE

"What you need . . .": Rivlin, "My Five Minutes with Bill Gates."

"My dear General . . .": Edmund S. Morgan, *The Genius of George Washington*, 5.

"You know, like . . .": Manes and Andrews, *Gates*, 105.

"He always wanted . . .": Manes and Andrews, *Gates*, 123.

"We would just. . .": Manes and Andrews, *Gates*, 104.

"It was kids . . .": Manes and Andrews, *Gates*, 299.

"Competing with Bill . . .": Manes and Andrews, *Gates*, 286.

"You couldn't take . . .": Manes and Andrews, *Gates*, 242.

CHAPTER TEN

For Gates's testimony and comments on it, see http://www.news. com/2100-1023-214993.html.

"proved time and . . .": http://www.windowsitpro.com/Article/ ArticleID/20269/20269.html.

"In Bill's eyes . . .": Isaacson, "In Search of the Real Bill Gates."

"feedback loop": Randall Stross, *The Microsoft Way*, 57.

"it was like . . .": http://news-service.stanford.edu/pr/98/981109 engelbart.html.

"If you can . . .": www.w3.org/People/Berners-Lee/Kids.

CHAPTER ELEVEN

"Bill and I . . .": Collins, "Backstory: Behind the Golden Gates."

"everyone agrees . . .": http://www.mtv.com/news/articles/1502402/ 20050516/id_0.jhtml.

"overworked": David Nasaw, *Andrew Carnegie*, 68.

"whatever I engage in . . .": David Nasaw, *Andrew Carnegie*, 113.

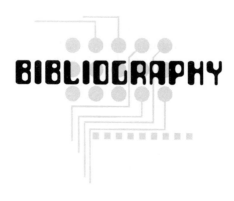

BIBLIOGRAPHY

Bardini, Thierry. *Boostrapping: Douglas Engelbart, Coevolution, and the Origins of Personal Computing.* Stanford: Stanford University Press, 2000.

Bock, Paula. "Principled & Pragmatic." *The Seattle Times*, January 26, 2003.

Collins, Clayton. "Backstory: Behind the Golden Gates." *Christian Science Monitor*, July 31, 2006.

"Dawn of the Ages of Robots." *Scientific American*, January, 2007, 58–65.

Gates, Bill. "A Q & A with Bill Gates." *The Seattle Times*, October 1, 2007.

Greene, Jay, et al. "Troubling Exits at Microsoft." *Business Week*, September 26, 2005.

Isaacson, Walter. "In Search of the Real Bill Gates." *Time* magazine, October 20, 2005.

Lohr, Steve. *Go To: The Story of the Math Majors, Bridge Players, Engineers, Chess Wizards, Maverick Scientists, and Iconoclasts, the Programmers Who Created the Software Revolution.* New York: Basic Books, 2001.

Manes, Stephen, and Paul Andrews. *Gates.* New York: Touchstone, 1993.

Markoff, John. *What the Dormouse Said: How the Sixties Counterculture Shaped the Personal Computer Industry.* New York: Penguin, 2005.

Morgan, Edmund S. *The Genius of George Washington.* New York: Norton, 1980.

Nasaw, David. *Andrew Carnegie.* New York: The Penguin Press, 2006.

"The New Powers in Giving." *The Economist,* July 1–7, 2006, 63–65.

Rich, Laura. *The Accidental Zillionaire: Demystifying Paul Allen.* Hoboken, N.J.: John Wiley, 2003.

Rivlin, Gary. "My Five Minutes with Bill Gates." Salon.com, July 6, 1999.

Stross, Randall E. "Digital Domain; What Is Google's Secret Weapon? An Army of Ph.D.'s." *New York Times,* June 6, 2004.

Stross, Randall E. *The Microsoft Way: The Real Story of How the Company Outsmarts Its Competition.* New York: Basic Books, 1997.

Wallace, James, and Jim Erickson. *Hard Drive: Bill Gates and the Making of the Microsoft Empire.* New York: HarperBusiness, 1992.

WEB SITES

http://informationweek.com/blog/main/archives/2007/05/bill_gates-yout.html
Michael Singer, "Bill Gates . . . YouTube Watcher, Zillow User."

http://www.gatesfoundation.org/AboutUs/
The Bill and Melinda Gates Foundation Web site is also useful.

http://www.microsoft.com/presspass/exec/billg/default.mspx
Microsoft's Web site contains a whole section devoted to speeches made by Bill Gates.

However, if you type "Bill Gates" or "Microsoft" into any search engine, you will soon land on sites that are dedicated to exposing him and his company, for example, http://www.microsuck.com/, or http://fakebill.wordpress.com/about/

I treat the speeches as public relations—crafted to serve Bill and his company—but sometimes containing valuable insights; I see the anti-Bill sites as their own form of advocacy, and you should carefully double check anything you read on them.

Browse through both sides, but then compare what you read with other sources, such as this book or the ones listed in the bibliography.

http:///www/w3.org/People/Berners-Lee/Kids
Tim Berners-Lee, "Answers for Young People."

INDEX

Note: Page numbers in *italics* indicate photos